Political Education in a Democracy

STUDENTS LIBRARY OF EDUCATION

GENERAL EDITOR:

J. W. Tibble
Emeritus Professor of Education
University of Leicester

EDITORIAL BOARD:

Psychology of Education:
Professor Ben Morris
University of Bristol

Philosophy of Education:
Professor Richard S. Peters
University of London

History of Education:
Professor Brian Simon
University of Leicester

Sociology of Education:
Professor William Taylor
University of Bristol

Volumes dealing with curriculum studies, methodology and other more general topics are the responsibility of the General Editor, Professor Tibble.

Political Education in a Democracy

Harold Entwistle

Department of Education
Sir George Williams University, Montreal

LONDON

ROUTLEDGE & KEGAN PAUL

*First published 1971
by Routledge & Kegan Paul Ltd
Broadway House, 68-74 Carter Lane
London EC4V 5EL
Printed in Great Britain by
Northumberland Press, Gateshead*

© *Harold Entwistle 1971*

No part of this book may be reproduced in any form without permission from the publisher, except for the quotation of brief passages in criticism

ISBN 0 7100 7132 9

THE STUDENTS LIBRARY OF EDUCATION has been designed to meet the needs of students of Education at Colleges of Education and at University Institutes and Departments. It will also be valuable for practising teachers and educationists. The series takes full account of the latest developments in teacher-training and of new methods and approaches in education. Separate volumes will provide authoritative and up-to-date accounts of the topics within the major fields of sociology, philosophy and history of education, educational psychology and method. Care has been taken that specialist topics are treated lucidly and usefully for the non-specialist reader. Altogether, the Students Library of Education will provide a comprehensive introduction and guide to anyone concerned with the study of education, and with educational theory and practice.

J. W. TIBBLE

Votes at eighteen, demands for participation in decision-making, and the activities of student and pupil radicals have all given prominence recently to the importance of educating future citizens for life in a democracy. Although recognition of this aspect of the work of the schools has been commonplace in educationists' pronouncements for many years, there have been relatively few systematic attempts to consider what 'education for democracy' means, and how it might be implemented within the schools. In the Colleges of Education there has been an almost complete neglect of political subjects. Against this background, Dr Entwistle's book assumes particular value. It analyses the relationships of concepts such as socialization and political education; it explains those aspects of the theory and practice of democracy that are particularly relevant

PREFACE

for schools, and it suggests ways in which teachers might better provide for the political education of their pupils. What Dr Entwistle has to say in this book is relevant as much for the teacher, or intending teacher in the primary school, as it is for the sixth-form teacher in the grammar or comprehensive school.

WILLIAM TAYLOR

Contents

1	Introduction	1
	The neglect of political education	1
	The need for political education	4
2	Political socialization or political education?	9
	Socialization, an ambiguous concept	9
	The educational value of the concept of political socialization	19
3	The limitations of traditional political education	24
	Its macro-orientation	24
	Its utopianism	25
	Its quietism	27
	Its theoretical bias	31
4	Pupil self-government: some theoretical considerations	34
	School democracy and the social context of the school	42
	School democracy and the rule of law	45
5	Practical political education	52
	Self-government in private and publicly maintained schools	52
	Mock activities	54
	School councils	58
	The school class	60
	Political education and voluntary groups in school	63

6 The meaning of democracy	68
Democracy in history	68
The limitations of parliamentary democracy	74
Associational democracy	76
Voluntary associations and government	78
Associational democracy and the concept of fraternity	84
Associational democracy and government by experts	90
Associational democracy and equality	92
Parliamentary and associational democracy	96
Voluntary associations and social class	97
Voluntary association and political education	100
7 Political theory and the curriculum	103
The primacy of the practical	103
The incidental approach to political theory	106
Civics	110
Political theory	111
8 Child development and political education	118
Political education as adult education	119
Political socialization and the child	120
Piaget on political development	122
Bibliography	127
Suggestions for further reading	135

1
Introduction

The neglect of political education

Although preparation for citizenship is an item in most statements of educational aims, political education has been neglected in schools in democratic societies. This paradox could be explained by the fact that whilst citizenship is often tacitly equated with political activity, it has also come to acquire a larger meaning than active participation in the political system. For example, comparative studies of the subject have tended to focus upon citizenship training as the development of a 'civic spirit' or 'civic loyalties'. The extensive inter-war studies of civic education in nine countries, analysed in Merriam's *The Making of Citizens*, showed schools to be preoccupied with national ideologies as the mainsprings of civic loyalty. A more recent study examined civics teaching in European schools mainly for its contribution towards inculcating 'the European civic spirit'. Amongst possible aims of civic education it notes development of 'a belief in the values of democratic institutions, laws and ways of life, and a sense of purpose in preserving and refining them' (Council for Cultural Co-operation, p. 20); but there is no consideration of democratic education as initiation into the skills and concepts required for active participation in political affairs. The document focuses, abstractly, upon notions of loyalty and belief, and the importance of learning 'to live together' (p. 17). And it concludes that 'the civic spirit is, in the last resort, a matter of loyalties, or at least a sense of identity with a particular society' (p. 30).

A somewhat different but equally broad conception of citizenship is implicit in textbooks of the 'English (or Mathematics) for Citizenship' variety. These tend to be concerned with activities like the use of banks, post offices, supermarkets, or the making of income tax returns and the completion of the numerous forms which the bureaucracy requires of the citizen. In this context, citizenship implies being a responsible husband or father, a discerning consumer, a conscientious worker and so on. Obviously many of these roles and activities have political implications, but political activity implies something more precise—a deliberate involvement within the political system intended to influence the workings of governmental institutions of various kinds. It is citizenship in this precise, political sense which is largely neglected by the schools.

Periodically, however, interest in political education erupts, usually at times of national or international crisis. In Britain, where observers have noted a tendency to neglect overtly political teaching (see Merriam; Gardner; Greenstein *et al.*, 1969), the period before and immediately following the Second World War was such a period of heightened interest in the training of citizens and the development of civics courses in schools. But by the mid-fifties, much of the sense of urgency for political education seemed to have diminished and, throughout the sixties, the increasing clamour for participation contrasted oddly with the neglect of political education in schools. As one political theorist puts it, the concern of educationists for 'the education of the whole man ... has not been expressed in a systematic attempt to inculcate an understanding of public affairs or to imbue the pupils with a desire to participate actively in the democratic process' (Robson, p. 31). This same writer found it odd that the British Newsom Report (concerned with the education of the average and less than average child) treated education for democracy in a manner that was 'pedestrian, narrow and unimaginative' (p. 38). This neglect of political education is underlined by the situation in teacher training: Heater found that not a single English college of education offered a course in political studies (pp. 142-4).

Mention of the democratic process points towards one explanation of this contemporary neglect of political education. From ancient times there has existed the conviction that one of the functions of the school is the education of rulers. Some of the outstanding classics of educational literature have been devoted to an examination of the ruler's function in different societies. Plato's *Republic*, Aristotle's *Politics*, Quintilian's *Orators*, Castiglione's *Book of the Courtier* and Elyot's *Governor*, all dealt explicitly with the nature of government in particular societies (ideal or real) and assessed its educational implications (see Harrison for an examination of this literature). However, in a tyranny or oligarchy the nature of this educational task is not difficult to define. Governors are few in number and what the state requires of them is capable of fairly precise definition. But in a democracy this is not so. In some sense everyone is supposed to govern. Moreover, democratic societies are not rigidly closed structures: they are societies open to change and development. Thus the task of evaluating governmental institutions, of making informed and intelligent political decisions and, consequently, of educating democratic citizens is much more difficult. It rules out any form of political education conceived in terms of fitting the individual for his place in society. One's place is a shifting location: it is implicit in the concept of equality of opportunity that there will be considerable social mobility. The concept of an open society also rules out any possibility of learning political participation by rule of thumb. Grasp of political principles is required if there is to be accommodation to change.

Towards the end of the nineteenth century there was a tardy recognition of the need for an educated citizenry.

INTRODUCTION

In Britain, closely following the enfranchisement of the industrial working class through the Reform Bill of 1867, the 1870 Education Act was introduced to the accompaniment of the cry 'We must educate our masters.' But despite the great changes which have been made in popular education in the past century, and considering the greater flexibility of the democratic society, it is apparent that the present day education of democratic citizens bears little comparison with the quality of the education traditionally available to the ruling class. A prominent American educationist has focused this dilemma of democratic education as follows:

> When we talk of our political goals, we admit the right of every man to be a ruler. When we talk of our educational problem, we see no inconsistency in saying that only a few have the capacity to get the education that rulers ought to have—either we should abandon the democratic ideal or we should help every citizen to acquire the education that is appropriate to free men (Hutchins, p. 44).

But, in the event, we are shy of the logic of Hutchins's conclusion. We still cling to the democratic ideal; but since our experience is that large numbers of people resist our attempts to cultivate that perceptive and rational temper of mind which democracy seems to require (see Almond and Verba, p. 474), we turn our backs on what appears to be an intractable problem. This essay is, in part, an attempt to articulate a concept of democracy which helps us off the horns of this dilemma and accommodates the different abilities, inclinations and enthusiasms of citizens in a democracy.

The need for political education

There is weighty research evidence that political involvement is correlated with length of full-time education even when the curriculum has probably contained no explicit political teaching (Almond and Verba, pp. 379-87; Lane, p.

472; Coleman, 1965, pp. 18-25; Dawson and Prewitt, pp 175-88; Key, 1964, Ch. 13). We might conclude from this evidence that in order to cultivate political awareness, what is required is not so much a programme of political studies and activities within the curriculum as the widespread extension of the period of compulsory schooling. Arguably, the greater political involvement and effectiveness of the better educated is a secondary effect of extended education: 'Education probably equips people with sufficient familiarity with general ideas and probably also with a sufficient supply of value preferences to enable them to respond to issues put in rather general terms. The less the education, the more directly must an issue bear upon a person's immediate interest or experience to evoke an opinion' (Key, loc. cit.). On this view, political maturity is a by-product of general education, not of teaching political theory.

However, the evidence is conflicting on the direction which the more active political participation of the better educated takes. Lipset argues that 'the higher one's education, the more likely one is to believe in democratic values and support democratic practices. All relevant studies indicate that education is far more significant than income or occupation' (p. 79). On the other hand, Key found that 'college education in some institutions may impart a liberal cast of mind; in others the effect may be quite the opposite' (op. cit., p. 379). The outcomes for citizenship of a longer education may be taken to be politically neutral; that is, 'level of education has a relationship to the "sense of citizen duty", the "sense of political efficacy", to psychological involvement' (Key, p. 324); but it cannot be assumed that this involvement will be personally disinterested, fraternal, devoted to the public good and generally in accordance with democratic values (see Almond and Verba, p. 382; Robson, p. 45). Indeed, Coleman points to the possibility 'that a predominantly scientific-technical emphasis in education is not in conflict with—indeed it possibly may be conducive to—a non-democratic pattern of political development'

(1966, p. 484). It does appear possible that personal development which is in accordance with democratic norms may depend upon the curriculum containing an explicitly political element.

However, it does not follow from the need for explicit political education that this ought to be provided in schools, particularly for the very young. Some would argue that political education is something which belongs to adult life when the individual has *become* a citizen (see Ch. 8 below). Given the importance of this insistence upon adult political education, one might conclude that the most effective political education is that which comes out of political participation itself. Voluntary associations have often been regarded as ideal training grounds for politicians. On this view, political wisdom and the mastery of the techniques of government are acquired through the practice of politics itself. Belief in the educative value of participation in the management of political institutions is to be observed throughout the history of democracy. Students of Greek democracy have emphasized that to be a member of the Athenian state was itself a political education. Zimmern argued that the whole climate of life in Athens, not merely its social and political institutions but even its architecture, was conducive to the political education of her citizens. Similar educational value from participation in political activity has been noted in connection with the early democratic settlements of the New World: 'In the town meeting the humblest citizen of Massachusetts could learn all about the management of public affairs' (Borgeaud, p. 154). Tocqueville also stressed the educational function of political associations in America: they were 'large free schools, where all the members of the community go to learn the general theory of association' (Vol II, p. 116). Again, historians of democracy in Britain have stressed the importance of membership of the early Methodist Church in training laymen for the responsible government of their religious societies and of contemporary non-religious associations (see Wearmouth). In turn, Trade Unions, Friendly Societies and Consumers' Co-operatives made their contribution towards the political education of working men.

Oakeshott has stressed the importance of this fact that political competence is acquired through the practice of politics itself. He has likened political education to learning how to participate in a conversation:

> There will always remain something of a mystery about how a tradition of political behaviour is learned, and perhaps the only certainty is that there is no point at which learning it can properly be said to begin. The politics of a community are not less individual (and not more so) than its language, and they are learned and practised in the same manner. We do not begin to learn our native language by learning the alphabet, or by learning its grammar; we do not begin by learning words, but words in use ... And this is also true of our political education ... The greater part—perhaps the most important part of our political education we acquire haphazard in finding our way about the world into which we are born, and there is no other way of acquiring it (p. 17; and see Crick, 1969, p. 6).

If it is true that a great deal of political wisdom is acquired thus, incidentally, through political activity itself, it seems that this diminishes the need for political education in schools. But there are a number of reasons for hesitating before seizing upon this complacent conclusion. In particular, it is evident that people cannot acquire political education as a by-product of political participation unless they first become active in politics. It is one thing to say that participation in government is itself educative: it is quite another matter to ensure that a large number of citizens is brought into an active relationship with those associations which are often held to provide the best schooling in politics. And clearly, mere membership of such a body is no guarantee of active participation in its affairs. From time to time it becomes public knowledge that decisions

INTRODUCTION

of great importance in associations (often having repercussions well beyond the membership itself) are taken with only a small minority of members present at meetings. Most people appear simply to be 'sleeping members' of the associations to which they belong. Active participation is not born merely out of membership: the disposition towards active responsible citizenship seems something which requires deliberate cultivation in an educational situation. Again, the political education acquired by those who become active within a voluntary association affords too narrow a perspective of the structure of modern government in its growing complexity. For this reason it is necessary that political concepts, institutions, traditions and values are first identified and structured, and then taught by those having the trained competence of mediating difficult skills to the young. Many of the human skills which could once be learned from life are now of a complexity which requires them to be deliberately taught by the school. In this respect, Oakeshott's analogy between learning political activity and learning a language is suggestive. There was a time when literacy was the prerogative of the learned professions and the average man could acquire his culture and engage in social relationships through the spoken word. But achievement of universal literacy seemed to require universal schooling. And although one's native language is still learned substantially in the home before schooling begins, the *mastery* of it in all its uses—literary, legal, technical, commercial, as well as conversational—depends upon its systematic study in schools and colleges. The higher standard of literacy required by an increasingly complex society involves the individual in a more systematic linguistic discipline than is possible through ordinary social intercourse. Similarly, the higher 'political literacy' demanded of a democratic citizen requires that the basic practical political education which participation in government itself undoubtedly provides should be enriched by the school.

2
Political socialization or political education?

Socialization, an ambiguous concept

Reflecting a shift in the interests of political theorists themselves (Guild and Palmer, p. 267), the development of political attitudes is more likely to be discussed nowadays by reference to the concept of political socialization than in more traditional terms of political education. From the United States in particular, there is a rapidly growing literature on political socialization (see additional reading). In some contexts, preference for the word 'socialization' appears to reflect nothing more than the jargon use of a trend word. Or the words 'education' and 'socialization' are used interchangeably, implying no distinction in meaning. For example, 'He [Plato] attributes the cyclical degeneration of politics to defects in political education; to failures in political socialization' (Dawson and Prewitt, p. 7; see also Newmann, p. 536). However, in other contexts, the preference for socialization over education is deliberate:

> both philosophers and practising politicians as long ago as Plato—and possibly long before that—have devoted thought and effort to the question of how to bring about such (i.e., political) engagement. Such practitioners and philosophers however, did not call the training process political socialisation; rather they called it civic education, lessons in patriotism, training for citizenship, or character training. Every one of these terms indicates that political values and attitudes are acquired, not in-

born—that they are the result of a learning process. The reason why we prefer to call this learning process political socialisation rather than civic education is that the latter has too deliberate a connotation. It presumes that system-appropriate political values are acquired as a result of deliberate indoctrination, textbook learning, conscious and rational weighing of political alternatives, and the like. It seems to assume that there is a definite point in time—a certain grade in school—when such learning can profitably start and a certain point when it is completed. This view is far too naïve and narrow; it completely ignores what we know about the way in which people go about 'learning' society's norms. For instance, it ignores the fact that much of this norm-internalisation goes on casually and imperceptibly—most of the time in fact without our ever being aware that it is going on. It proceeds so smoothly precisely because we are unaware of it. We take the norms for granted, and it does not occur to us to question them (Sigel, pp. 79-80; see also Rieselbach and Balch, p. 74).

Apart from illustrating the point that some writers deliberately prefer the word socialization, this extract has been quoted at length because it epitomizes the value of the concept of socialization to educationists whilst, at the same time, underlining the reason why writers in the past have seen the idea of education to be a necessary part of our conceptual equipment in picking out learning experiences of a particular kind and quality. If two millennia of educationists have been as narrow and naïve as Sigel believes, then her warning about the limitations of deliberate teaching of social norms is timely. (In passing it is worth noting that the term education carries no assumptions about age or grade limits for different types of learning, and few contemporary educationists—if any—would assume it did: on this point, at least, Sigel is erecting a straw man.) But is this change in terminology justified merely as a preference for a word which indicates a less deliberate approach towards learning and teaching? Do socialization and education pick out different technical approaches to learning, alternative methodologies, or is there a qualitative difference in these processes which makes it necessary to retain the notion of political or civic *education* in our vocabulary of child-rearing. The last sentence in the quotation seems to hold the key to such a qualitative difference: the concept of education requires something more than a process of learning norms, attitudes and skills without asking questions about them. We shall return to this point later.

But even at the technical level, the difference between the process of socialization and that of education does not mark the kind of distinction which Sigel implies. It is quite possible for teaching and learning in an educational situation to have a non-deliberate, haphazard, incidental appearance, at least from the viewpoint of the learner. Sigel's emphasis upon socialization-type learning is made partly with reference to the assumed greater effectiveness of incidental learning: 'Important though deliberate indoctrination is, it is probable that incidental learning—precisely because it is incidental—has a more lasting effect on the acquisition of political values and behaviour' (Sigel, p. 81). However, even supposing that the superiority of incidental, discovery learning had been empirically demonstrated beyond any reasonable doubt, it is not possible to distinguish socialization from education in these terms. To say that education is a deliberate process is only to talk about the intention of the educator, not about his methodology. Educators often do have well defined objectives and they choose the methodology most likely to achieve what they set out to do. But their methods need not be deliberate in the sense of being ceremoniously ostensive or didactic. 'Incidental learning can be acquired in the course of overhearing adult conversation' (Sigel, p. 81). But adults can *intend* to be overheard by children. What is intentional from the teacher's point of view may appear quite incidental to the learner. A deliberate intention may be operationalized in the school in a way which has all the appearance of being an offhand, unconsidered afterthought, so that from the child's point of view his learning may appear self-activated. This, indeed, is part of the rationale of progressive education. Rousseau's Emile stumbled through his childhood apparently learning everything incidentally, discovering the universe for himself; but one recalls Rousseau's prescription: 'Never let him use a word you have not anticipated or do anything you have not foreseen.' Nor is this apparently unstructured, incidental form of teaching all that novel. Plato also advised, 'Let your children's lessons take the form of play'; in early years, informal learning characterized even the civic education of the philosopher kings. Thus, the concept of socialization is in no way essential to reminding us as teachers that our work may be the more effective when it employs methods which to the learner seem casual and haphazard, giving him the impression that he is the agent of his own education.

But here we face a moral question. What justification have we for concealing from children—whether as parents or teachers—our real intentions? And what, as educationists, do we have to say to the complacent conclusion that the process of socialization leaves us in the position of taking norms for granted without it ever occurring to us to question them? Or again, what ought to be our reaction to the preference for the idea of socialization over education when political socialization is defined as 'the internalisation within the individual of *another's views*'? (Hyman, p. 95, my italics). Can educationists be satisfied with the conclusion that people should live in borrowed political clothes, since the concept of education requires the development of personal autonomy and a capacity to think for oneself? Of course, perhaps those who want to discard entirely the concept of political education are realistically inferring from the fact that many people do not develop individual autonomy, the conclusion that it is pointless for the schools to focus on that sort of objective. On the other hand, the observation that it does not occur to us

SOCIALIZATION OR POLITICAL EDUCATION?

to question the political norms into which we are socialized (without even the qualifying condition, 'most men' or 'the average man') evidently flies in the face of experience. As a statement of fact it is falsified by the current turbulent and violent student protest against many of our political and social norms. But this also raises the more important ethical point. Supposing most people do merely internalize, unquestioningly, the norms they find in their social environment, would this be a state of affairs upon which we would want to offer no evaluative comment? Even leaving aside the point that many student activists are probably questioning the political and economic norms of Western, free enterprise societies which most of their citizens accept with little question, it is also a fact that many more 'ordinary' citizens strike political attitudes and express beliefs which question the social and economic *status quo* in these traditional societies (see pp. 97-100 below). Moreover, as citizens we are often racialists, chauvinists, intolerant of minorities, dedicated to class war, deferential towards those who seem born to govern or, alternatively, suspicious of *them* and convinced that politics is a dirty game, the profession of knaves. As an extreme example of this hostile socialization towards politicians, most texts on political socialization cite Wylie's observation that children in the Vaucluse region of France constantly hear adults referring to governments as sources of evil and to politicians as instruments of evil (see Hodgetts, pp. 78-80, for similar cynical views of politicians expressed by Canadian pupils). The unsatisfactory outcome of political socialization for intelligent, sympathetic and informed political participation is summarized by Hess and Torney:

> These early perceptions, images and concepts are sometimes trusting and naïve, sometimes cynical, often amusing, and frequently inaccurate and distorted. Yet they are much more than children's playful fantasy—they are characteristic of a period in which children become

oriented towards the values, beliefs, knowledge, and opinions of the political culture, and they provide the basis for later behaviour as adult citizens (p. 1).

In the face of this sort of evidence about the direction which political socialization often takes, it is odd that there are those who discount the need for education and appear satisfied with socialization which results in unquestioning acceptance of 'the norms, attitudes and behaviour accepted by the ongoing political system' (Sigel, p. 78). One has to write 'appear satisfied' since this particular tradition of political theory is curiously ambiguous, not least in relation to political values. Sigel, for example, sees nothing odd or disturbing in her conclusion that 'the net over-all effect of political socialisation is in the direction of supporting the *status quo*, or at least the major aspects of the existing political regime ... *and therein lies its significance for the political-system survival and stability*' (p. 88, my italics) when juxtaposed with her earlier example of the Negro child socialized by his experience to accept passively and indifferently 'that discrimination is condoned by wide sectors of American life' (p. 82). No doubt the stability of the American political system (a primary value for most writers on political socialization) depends upon this acquiescence of the disadvantaged, but it is not clear how far Sigel's conclusion that 'it is quite possible that the political lesson learned from life experience of such a youngster will be that the safest way to get along is to be politically non-engaged, passive and indifferent' (op. cit., p. 82) represents the writer's one view of what would be desirable behaviour from the disadvantaged, or whether she is merely stating the direction which the socialization of Negroes has usually taken in the past. Certainly, Litt's examination of civics textbooks and programmes used in schools in the Boston area with different socio-economic groups revealed that their contents seemed deliberately designed to reinforce the differential political orientations of those groups:

Students in the different communities are being trained to play different political roles and to respond to political phenomena in different ways. In the working class community, where political involvement is low, the arena of civic education offers training in the basic democratic procedures without stressing political participation or the citizen's view of conflict and disagreement as indigenous to the political system. Only in the affluent and politically vibrant community (Alpha) are insights into political processes and functions of politics passed on to those who, judging from their socio-economic and political environment, will likely man those positions that involve them in influencing or making political decisions (p. 492).

Similarly, from his study of the socialization of British secondary school students, Abramson suspected that, like the Boston children, 'British children in non-selective schools are taught to accept relatively non-participatory roles in the political system', whilst 'teachers assume that public schoolboys and grammar school sixth formers may attain leadership roles in the society and the polity' (see also Gardner, p. 44). The stability of the American (or any other) political system may, indeed, depend upon widespread indifference or deference on the part of those against whom there is social or economic discrimination, but the increasing tendency of these not to accept their lot without question is evidence of a failure of many to learn the lesson required by a stable democratic system, namely, that its members 'are expected to learn to effect change through elections, through the application of group practice, rather than through riots or revolution' (op. cit., p. 178). A proper conclusion from this sort of threat to the stability of Western political systems would be that the process of political socialization frequently (and increasingly) flies in the face of any concept of social justice.

To mention an ethical concept like social justice may be to invite the response that one has simply missed the point of the socialization literature. The intention of these writers is not to justify socialization which results in a resigned acceptance of one's status in life, but merely to collect evidence on how people do, in fact, develop their political orientations in the particular populations covered by their research. They are concerned with what *is*, not with prescriptive political theory and questions of what ought to be. In a different political universe, socialization might be different, but in the places they have looked, this is the way it happens. However, such a rebuttal would be disingenuous. For the literature of political socialization displays considerable ambiguity with reference to this problem of the relationship between fact and value. Dawson and Prewitt, for example, are explicit in rejecting any evaluative intention: 'We are avoiding normative questions ... we do not discuss here whether what we identify as central tendencies are the most "appropriate" or "efficient" pattern of socialisation and whether such a pattern is beneficial or detrimental' (p. 203).

However, despite this sort of avowal of normative neutrality and of intention only to explain what actually does happen, there is considerable use in this literature of value-impregnated concepts. Take, for example, the frequent references to political *stability*, which is usually assumed to be a consequence of satisfactory socialization (Dawson and Prewitt, p. 61; Sigel, loc. cit.; Almond and Verba, Ch. 15). The assumption is that stable political systems derive their stability from the modes of socialization experienced by the young. (Dawson and Prewitt, p. 61). But what sense are we to read into their use of the word 'stability' in this context? It may be claimed that usage in the political socialization literature is purely descriptive. That is, the term 'stable political system' is used non-evaluatively merely to pick out a certain kind of system (the stable) from a different sort (the unstable): nothing is being claimed for the superiority of the former over the latter. But if the word is to be understood as having a simple descriptive force, this ought to be made explicit. Otherwise, ambiguity is in-

SOCIALIZATION OR POLITICAL EDUCATION?

evitable in view of the widespread assumption in social disciplines like economics, psychology and politics that stability constitutes a desirable state of affairs. In these areas the word frequently has a normative sense. An individual's stability is an index of his mental health; economic stability (e.g., the preference for a fixed rather than a floating exchange rate between currencies, and the avoidance of extreme cyclical fluctuations in the level of economic activity) is the objective of governments and monetary authorities; the existence of political stability in a state is usually a criterion for international investment and the absence of it a justification for foreign intervention in revolutionary situations. And despite the ambiguity of their position, the political socialization theorists do seem committed to political stability as a desirable state of affairs. For example, 'humans must learn their political behaviour early and well and persist in it. Otherwise there would be no regularity—perhaps even chaos' (Hyman, p. 17). Given the second sentence, the force of 'must' in this passage seems clearly prescriptive. Or again, in the following passage from Dawson and Prewitt (who, as we have seen, are categorical about the non-prescriptive function of their analysis), the words and passages italicized appear to carry clear evaluative implications:

> In stable polities, the *strength* and *durability* of basic orientations such as national identification, patriotism, and attachment to rules, ways of doing things and ideologies provide a *firm* and *stable* underpinning for the *fundamental forms and goals* of the government. They make for *continuity* and *intergenerational agreement* in the political culture. Governments and political leaders can gauge and predict citizen reactions and expectations. If such basic attachments were acquired only later in life and were more *capricious*, it would be more difficult to establish and maintain *a stable political culture* and *orderly* political procedures (p. 61).

Perhaps this passage explains why some political socialization theorists wish to diminish the importance of political education which, by definition, would lead to questioning of political norms and, hence, be a threat to political stability and the *status quo*. In wishing to minimize the effects of political education and hence the need for initiation into rational strategies for promoting change, and through their assumption that socialization disposes us to take our political orientations for granted without questioning them (a good thing in the interests of political stability), or that the best strategy for dealing with conflict may be to remain passive and indifferent, the political socialization theorists are clearly opting for irrationality, political quietism and the values of the *status quo*—a tenable position, no doubt, but no less a judgment of value than that of those who prefer to stress political education and believe in the possibility of the improvement of political intelligence and moral sensibility.

So far as our socialized dispositions are apt to dispose us to the view that (in Hobbes's phrase) life is 'poore, nasty, brutish and shorte', it would seem that personal self-respect points towards the need for the education (i.e., improvement) of our political skills and attitudes. To question the value of deliberate attempts to refine men's political perceptions is to see little dignity in the human condition, and to ascribe to the average citizen only a capacity for prejudice, chauvinism and political naïvety. It is also probably to take an elitist and essentially non-democratic view of politics since, evidently, socialization works for some in a way which ensures a perception of the political system which makes access to power and authority over their fellow men easy to achieve if they wish it.

In fact, the conclusion in Western democracies that socialization of the young is a guarantee of political stability is increasingly untenable. In the special issue of the *Harvard Educational Review* (1968), 'Political Socialisation', there emerges a critique of the complacent conclusions of much of the socialization literature (Jennings and Niemi, Litt, Hess). Hess, whose own work on political socialization is well known, argues that 'since it assumes stability and concensus in the adult population, political socialisation is a concept which it is difficult to apply during periods of rapid change and of open conflict between major segments of a society. It is of little usefulness in the United States today' (1968). He faults socialization, as it has been practised in America, on the grounds that 'the schools have contributed to divisions within society by teaching a view of the nation and its political processes which is incomplete and simplistic, stressing values and ideals but ignoring social realities'. He concludes that 'it is no longer effective, perhaps, to think of socialisation in terms of transmitting the norms of the system; a more useful perspective is the teaching of principles which underlie the normative statements'. Although he does not bring himself to use the word, Hess is really prescribing political *education*.

The educational value of the concept of political socialization

However, to talk about the possibility of political education raising the level of intelligence, morality and skill with which citizens view the political system is to take an act of faith. As we observed earlier, political education in the past (so far as it has ever really been tried) has not been highly successful in achieving this objective. No doubt one of the reasons for this is that deliberate civic education in schools has had to make its way against the socialized dispositions which the young bring with them to school. So far as those who emphasize political socialization have shown that political orientations occur earlier than has often been imagined, their findings cannot be ignored by educationists. The emphasis upon early political socialization is a necessary reminder that any attempt to educate children politically must confront them as persons having already acquired certain attitudes, skills, and cognitive structures which dispose them to see the political universe in a particular way. Even the youngest children are not politically innocent when they come into school: 'Every piece of evidence indicates that the child's political world begins to take shape well before he even enters elementary school and that it undergoes the most rapid change during those years' (Easton and Hess, p. 235). (But see Hodgett's warning against generalizing from American evidence on early political socialization in view of the unique preoccupation of American schools with daily patriotic rituals —note 6, p. 9; see also Easton and Dennis, Ch. 19, for a discussion of the applicability of American political socialization research, 'Beyond the American System'.) Thus, teachers of politics are not writing political facts and ideas upon a *tabula rasa*, and sociologists have recently been performing a useful service in insisting that, in order to be effective, educational procedures must take account of the way in which the child is acculturized apart from his experience in school. Influenced by this growing literature on socialization, even official reports on education (e.g., Newsom) begin from the assumption that children from some social environments may be near ineducable when they get to school. Bernstein, for example, has popularized the notion that children from lower working class environments may speak a language whose syntax is quite different from that normally required by the traditional school. In the same way, those who argue the greater efficacy of political socialization over deliberate attempts to provide political education are making the useful point that children often learn from their social environment a language of politics which differs from the rational and academic discourse of political theorists. Moreover, children will have differing political orientations correlating with differences in sex (Hyman, p. 30-3; Greenstein, 1965, Ch. 6; Easton and Dennis, pp. 343-9), social class (Greenstein, 1965; Litt, Ch. 5), socio-economic status (Greenstein, 1965, p. 106; Easton and Dennis, pp. 343-9), personality type (Eysenck; Adorno) and family background. Both family political commitment and the liberality or otherwise of the discipline of the home are assumed to influence political orientation (Greenstein, 1965, pp. 44, 155; Gardner, pp. 33-5; Hyman, Ch. 4; Robson, p. 30). Moreover, the authority rituals of the school itself are a potent sources of political socialization. (Crosby, p. 129; Dawson and Prewitt, p. 155-8). Whatever the manifest ideology of the society itself, the discipline and ritual life of the school may reinforce attitudes which are authoritarian, discriminatory, deferential and even delinquent, as opposed to those which are liberal or democratic.

Empirical evidence of this sort provides some justification for the conclusions of those teachers whose experiences teach them that attempts to counter the illiberal, prejudiced, misinformed socialization which occurs outside the school can only be partially successful. One of the values of the stress upon socialization is the reminder that formal and deliberate teaching of political norms and skills will not necessarily develop either rational thought, liberal and tolerant inter-personal and group attitudes, or political commitment (see Dawson and Prewitt, pp. 148-55). Gardner cites Azreal's conclusion 'that the reaction of a large percentage of Soviet pupils to political education was indifference and apathy' (pp. 41-2). Kazamias and Massialas quote German evidence that 'a course in civics, even if taught by a good teacher, does not have any penetrating influence upon the political consciousness of students' (p. 134). They conclude that these findings would generally be supported by American research and there is some evidence for this in Remmers. Contributors to his collection of studies report conflicting evidence on the effects of school climates and civic teaching upon political and social attitudes. Corder reported 'the prevalence of unfavourable minority group attitudes' amongst teenagers. Horton reported that 'a significant proportion of the nation's high school seniors does not agree with the freedoms guaranteed by the Bill of Rights'; moreover, belief in democratic values, in terms of having taken a school course in U.S. Government or Civics, showed no constructive effect attributable to such courses. The argument of our next chapter will be that this past failure of political education may well be a function of the inadequacy of traditional teaching of civics, and Horton did concede that the ineffectiveness of civics may relate to the fact that courses in this subject 'concentrate more upon the mechanics of government than upon the *values* of democracy' (see also Hodgetts, especially Chs. 2 and 4). Other studies reported by Kirsch and by Mainer did point to more optimistic conclusions. Kirsch, for example, concluded that 'knowledge of democratic principles reduces social distance.'

But, whatever the reason, it is clear that successful political education is not easy to achieve. However, in this respect the teaching of politics is no different from that of any other subject in having to assimilate the attitudes and knowledge which learners have already acquired, and in often running counter to the child's experiences. Teachers of politics are only in a similar position to teachers of science, for example, or the arts. Piaget has shown that our early scientific orientations are tainted with animism, artificialism, and assumptions of magic (1967). Similarly, attempts at aesthetic education frequently encounter attitudes towards art which are philistine and tasteless. In all areas of the curriculum, from early socialization, children will be disposed to take an idiosyncratic and often irrational or insensitive view of scientific, aesthetic, religious and even mathematical concepts. But we conduct the educational enterprise in schools from the conviction that however much one man's meat may be another's poison, to be receiving education is to be moving towards a better informed, rational and sensitive viewpoint upon the universe in which we live. Clouded by our socialized perceptions and dispositions, our education may vouchsafe us only a partial insight into the nature of things and institutions ('we see through a glass darkly'), but the teacher's assumption must be that we ought to attempt this refinement of our

SOCIALIZATION OR POLITICAL EDUCATION?

perceptions, which the concept of education requires. And the political segment of our universe is neither more nor less difficult of access in these terms than is any other.

The argument of this chapter has been that the concept of political socialization is a valuable corrective to naïve assumptions that a rational and altruistic political theory has only to be implanted to take root in the friendly soil of the child's mind before fructifying in responsible and informed political activity. This emphasis upon socialization is a necessary reminder that any deliberate attempt at political education in the schools will occur relatively late in the learner's experience, given what evidence we have on early orientation towards political ideas and symbols. Further, research into the way in which people *do* acquire their political orientations, fortuitously, from the environment ought to contribute towards our understanding of how we should set about the task of educating political values and skills. As Dawson and Prewitt put it: 'Issues of political violence, governmental deception, aggressive national behaviour, social stagnation, or racial injustice, will be better understood when we have become more knowledgeable about political socialisation' (p. 14). But given the urgency of some of these problems, and our knowledge that prevalent attitudes towards them are frequently inconsistent with our democratic values, political education cannot await the outcome of massive research programmes into the anatomy of some of these near-intractable social issues. Moreover, the moral ambiguity of the concept of political socialization, as revealed by the literature, requires that we also have recourse to a concept which unambiguously requires the notion that our child-rearing practices should be value-directed and concerned with the improvement of our political culture. Hence, to distinguish political education from the wider area of socialization is unavoidable and is a distinction which helps to clarify our analysis at a number of points in subsequent chapters.

3
The limitations of traditional political education

Its macro-orientation

Perhaps the contemporary neglect of political education follows, as much as anything, from dissatisfaction with the manner in which it has been conducted in the past. Usually, courses in civics have been concerned with macro-politics. They have been parliamentary-oriented in countries governed through British parliamentary institutions whilst, in the United States, civics teaching has had a presidential and congressional orientation. Citizenship has been represented as involvement with these macro-governmental institutions, essentially as a voter in elections. Indeed, *the vote* is taken to be the epitome of democratic citizenship: 'an "ideal" citizen [would be] one who used his vote effectively to reward and punish public servants' (Greenstein, 1965, p. 57; and see Hess and Torney, pp. 60-1, 212). In particular, much of the recent American literature on political socialization reinforces this view that political education has been concerned primarily with macro-politics. Despite occasional reference to the pluralist nature of democratic society and acknowledgment of the importance of interest groups in democratic political systems, this research has confined itself almost exclusively to examination of children's perceptions of political figures like congressmen, state governors and, especially, the president (see

Hess and Torney; Greenstein, 1965, 1966; Dawson and Prewitt; Jennings and Niemi; Lane; Easton and Dennis). Examinations of English children's political conceptions display a similar macro-orientation in focusing entirely upon their perceptions of national political leaders (Jackson; Greenstein, 1969; Crick, 1969). And a recent study epitomizes civics education in Canada as concerned with 'nice, neat little Acts of Parliament' (Hodgetts, pp. 19-21).

It is a major theme of this essay that the macro approach to political education is unsound in providing a sociologically erroneous account of how the democratic citizen can and does function most actively and satisfactorily (to himself) within the body politic. The political system comprehends more than congressional and parliamentary institutions, and the citizen's involvement with these national institutions of government is more likely to be mediated through micro-institutions of various kinds, than directly through the franchise or by individual communication with members of the executive or the legislature. This point and its educational implications will be elaborated in Chapter 6.

Its utopianism

However, the questionable political sociology of the traditional civics course in only one aspect of the discontinuity between the theoretical teaching of the school and the practice of politics outside. There is also a utopian note in traditional civics. The myth of *the vote* as an expression of an individual's rational reflection upon the problems of politics is difficult to sustain by reference to the psychology of political behaviour itself:

> An oversimplified view of how our democracy works is to conceive of all voters as independent individuals considering the candidates and issues and voting accordingly. A somewhat more sophisticated view is the picture of political parties in contention, with each person accepting a package of candidates and policies. The reality is much

more complicated, with a vast number of organised groups exerting many kinds of pressure (Kerber and Smith, p. 296; see also Hodgetts, p. 30).

As Lewin put it: 'traditionally democratic theory ... demands more of the individual citizen than he can realistically fulfil and promises more than can be delivered' (quoted Patterson, 1965, p. 89). In thus oversimplifying the processes and demands of democratic government, traditional civics is preaching a doctrine rather than explaining the mechanism of political institutions or the political motivation of citizens. The message is that this is how institutions would work and how citizens would behave in the best of all possible political worlds. As we shall presently argue, the ethical foundations of democratic society must form part of any syllabus of political education (see Chapters 6 and 7). But one of our arguments will also be that the utopia of classical macro-political theory (e.g., the eulogy of parliamentary democracy) is not the universe in which the active citizen would wish to live. The current clamour for participation is clearly a vote of little confidence in the traditional conception of the democratic citizen fulfilling his proper role merely as a voter. It indicates that the citizen finds little congruence between the ideology of traditional civics and the facts of life as he finds them in the political system. A gap between theory and practice is as evident in our past attempts at political education as it often also is in our professional and technical education. The cynical attitude towards theory which this discontinuity produces could be diminished by a more accurate theoretical explanation of the processes and opportunities of politics.

No doubt one reason for this resort to utopianism is the belief that the initiate into any activity ought not, at the outset, to be confronted with the compromises, tragedies and disappointments which characterize a great deal of life outside the school. The world is a pretty sordid place in which to live, but (as we have noted already) teaching involves a commitment to ethical valuation of how the world ought to be. The political system may be a jungle, but perhaps the young ought to be reminded of traditions of political and social philosophy which enjoin men to discover institutions for the realization of their better selves. They discover soon enough that experience constantly falsifies utopian expectations. But as well as moral considerations, there is the psychological question of how far the child's sense of security can only be nourished by confronting him with a benevolently ordered universe:

> Some adults—and there is reason to believe they are numerous—feel it is inappropriate to let the child know about what is often felt to be the seamy and contentious side of politics. He is too young, he will not understand, it will disillusion him too soon, awareness of conflict among adults will be disturbing, are some of the arguments raised against telling the whole truth (Easton and Hess).

Easton and Hess themselves conclude, however, that

> in spite of these forces working in the direction of idealisation, our data do suggest that, contradictory as it may seem, at least in some areas the child is quite capable of facing up to the passions and conflict in political life and that he is equally capable of tolerating such stress without succumbing either to cynicism or to disenchantment with political authority.

This empirically-based conclusion would support Crick's assumption that 'a political education should be realistic and should chasten the idealist. Ideas are too important to be embalmed, they must be wrestled with and confronted, but fairly and openly' (1969, p. 12).

Its quietism

It is far from clear why theory is so often at odds with

practice. As we have already implied, one reason is that teachers of theory often assume the role of missionary. Since the ways in which we do actually organize our affairs leaves a great deal to be desired, we teach an 'ideal' theory as a challenge to change. But in political education our indoctrination may stem from less commendable motives. Whether intended or not, there is a quietist persuasion in a great deal of civics. We noted in our introduction (p. 1) that political education has emphasized civic *loyalty*, a norm often considered incompatible with criticism which seems to be 'rocking the boat'. The doctrine of government by consent and the mystique attached to the privilege of voting in quadrenniel or quinquenniel national elections, also seem an invitation to desist from active participation in the interval.

American students of political socialization have underlined this quietist, non-participant, deferential dimension of political education, with its focus upon *authority* rather than upon *participation*: 'Compliance to rules and authority is the major focus of civics education in the elementary schools ... the citizen's right to participate in government is not emphasised in the school curriculum. The importance placed upon the citizen's active participation shows a pattern different from the emphasis placed upon attachment to the country and compliance to law' (Hess and Torney, pp. 110-11). A publication of the English Ministry of Education, *Citizens Growing Up*, defined the good citizen as one displaying 'humility, service, restraint and respect for personality'. From this kind of official guideline, it is not surprising that an American observer of English schools found that 'the majority of teachers were far more interested in including within the formal curriculum content congruent with a subject (i.e., passive) rather than a citizen (i.e., active) model' (Gardner). This persuasion towards a passive political role is also related to the macro-orientation of traditional civics. It is not merely that the average man's role is essentially passive consequent upon the lengthy interval between elections and legislatures: it is also related to the idealization of national authorities like presidents and monarchs. Thus, in the U.S.A., the child's perception of the President is that of a benign and competent provider: 'The child's first relationship is with the President whom he sees in highly positive terms. This indicates his basic trust in the benevolence of government. Young children relate to the President as to figures they know personally, expressing strong emotional attachment to him and expecting protection from him' (Hess and Torney, pp. 46-7; see also Greenstein, 1965, p. 154; Easton and Dennis, Ch. 8). And even when, with age and experience of personal fallibility in particular presidents, the child develops attachments to the *presidency* rather than the president, his essential trust 'in the benign qualities of political authority sets a level of expectation that is never completely abandoned' (Hess and Torney, p. 55; see also Easton and Dennis, p. 204).

A recent study of English children found that they acquire similar perceptions of the Queen (but not of the Prime Minister) as an essentially sympathetic and benevolent figure (Greenstein, 1969). Easton and Dennis conclude from their own research that

> the small child sees a vision of holiness when he chances to glance towards government—a sanctity and rightness of the demigoddess who dispenses the milk of human kindness. The government protects us, helps us, is good, and cares for us when we are in need (p. 137).

It is expecting a great deal of the school to upset such a sense of security in the stability afforded by political institutions and authorities, by urging participant interference in the way the country is governed.

Indeed, the dominantly quietist emphasis in citizenship training, enjoining obedience to rules and respect for authority, should occasion little surprise. Popular education had its origins in a social philosophy of civilizing the masses just sufficiently to teach them their place, whilst taking care not to give them ideas above their station in life. Today, this function of the educational system is rarely as explicitly stated as it was in early nineteenth-century educational debates in the British parliament, though an implication of 'education for obedience' has been detected by one English critic of some curriculum developments on behalf of the young school leaver (White), and it is implicit in much criticism of American education in the Negro ghettos. It is true that most educationists and teachers do pay lip service to a more liberal ideal: 'the full development of persons' is a commonplace, if vacuous, educational aim. Nevertheless, to the radical student movement, the teacher is the tool (however unwittingly) of the power structure in capitalist society dedicated to the education of compliant consumers. The teacher is also likely to be a supporter of one of the traditional political parties, thus having a vested interest in preservation of the system of party politics. There is not room here to explore the implications of this view of the teacher as prisoner of the system he serves. But other ambiguities of the teacher's role are relevant to explaining the departure from reality of traditional civics. In order to avoid unacceptable bias and the dangers of indoctrination, teaching academic disciplines requires commitment to dispassionate and disinterested examination of relevant data. Hence the preoccupation of civics with political procedures, with tradition, with political participation as a detached Olympian procedure of standing in rational judgment upon politicians (voting after weighing the pros and cons) rather than commending commitment to the daily compromising engagement that political activity really is. And in the publicly maintained school this dilemma is a real one. Here the alternative to academic detachment may appear to be espousal of causes or activities which, given the normative plurality of democratic societies, command no universal consent from the community at large (Entwistle, 1970, pp. 38-46; see also Cohen for a discussion of the problem of bias in political education).

Its theoretical bias

Apart from its questionable sociology, traditional civics has the further, almost inevitable, limitation of being primarily a theoretical activity. Indeed, it is one of the difficulties of a macro-oriented political education that it can only be approached theoretically. It cannot provide the practical experiences which are required either to concretize the theory or to lead to mastery of political machinery. Hence, political education has been largely a matter of teaching *about* the processes of government. Clearly, if democratic citizenship is characterized by voting in presidential, congressional, parliamentary and even local elections, then the child can only be invited to contemplate political activity as a spectator. In no sense can he practise or test what is taught. In this connection, a major hindrance to the development of political education in schools appears to be the inability of the immature to understand —or to want to make the effort to understand—the theory and practice of politics, whose data seems drawn inevitably from an alien adult world. One of the problems of macrocentred education for citizenship is that it must be conceived entirely as a preparation for activity which is only a distant prospect for the child. Hence, the immediate practical application of what is learned must always lie in mere 'exercises' in mock situations, never in activities of real present concern for children. The notion that education is a preparation for life is not necessarily inconsistent with the view that schooling should have present meaning for the child (Entwistle, 1970, Ch. 5). But presently meaningful education is only consistent with preparation, if the concepts and skills which children are acquiring are capable both of present application and of development into more sophisticated concepts and higher order principles.

THE LIMITATIONS OF POLITICAL EDUCATION

The problem with parliamentary-oriented political education is that it provides no possibility of developing an understanding of political institutions and principles from appropriate activity having meaning for the child. Political education of this kind must necessarily proceed, not by way of development from the simple to the complex, but by a process of 'watering down' concepts and skills only appropriate to adult life. This creates problems of motivation, since the way of life it mediates is utterly alien to the child: it touches him only through the political concern of the adults he knows (and these may themselves be little involved or aware of political activity), not in terms of matters of vital concern to himself.

The child is further alienated from this adult-centred macro-orientation of civics because of the almost inevitable resort to purely descriptive teaching *about* the process of government. Because the child cannot be actively involved with the data of political theory in the manner necessary to cultivate principled understanding, he is confronted with an arid collection of facts about eligibility to vote, the relationship of executive to legislature to judiciary, the roles of presidents or prime ministers or monarchs, how bills pass through legislatures, the functions of political oddities like Black Rod and so on—sterile descriptions about which most children could not care less, because literally sterile in the sense of incapable of fertilizing either his experience or his imagination.

As Patterson argues, political education for the young requires a different approach:

> Part of our task is to recognise that there are structures of knowledge realistically pertinent to the idea of citizenship at every level of individual learning ... and intellectual honesty about the political process in any of its myriad forms captures the essential excitement of the subject. Children, for good reason, often find the social studies a crashing bore because we empty the subject

of its natural vitality before making it available (1965, p. 91).

This recalls Bruner's hypothesis 'that any subject can be taught effectively in some intellectually honest form at any stage of development' (p. 12), a conviction stemming from his assumption that 'the basic ideas that lie at the heart of all science and mathematics and the basic themes that give form to life and literature are as simple as they are powerful' (p. 33). If Bruner is correct in this assumption, there ought to be no insuperable obstacle to devising a programme of political education which fires the imagination of children. Unfortunately, as I have demonstrated elsewhere, political theorists themselves are often less than sanguine about the possibility of devising a civics syllabus which is anything more than an arid description of political institutions (1969).

The dilemma of political education is often reflected in the attitudes of those who teach that vast majority of children who will end their formal education at the statutory leaving age, when a significant gap still remains between the end of schooling and the legal age of citizenship. Often conceding that the macro-political content of traditional civics is premature with young adolescents they ask, 'But if we don't prepare them to vote, who else will?' This concern for the future citizenship of the average child is to be commended. It deserves to promote attempts to articulate a concept of political education which begins with the 'political' interests of children themselves, whilst providing a basis of knowledge and skill appropriate to the more sophisticated political participation available to the adult citizen.

4
Pupil self-government: some theoretical considerations

In Chapter 2 we noted how discussion of the school as an agent of political orientation tended to focus on the socializing function of its disciplinary rituals, rather than upon the manifest educational function of its curriculum. This disciplinary ethos seemed authority-centred and in Chapter 3 evidence was cited for the view that such an orientation encouraged a quietist conception of political participation, emphasizing the individual's role as subject rather than as active citizen. From this sort of assumption about the direction of political socialization in the traditional school, there has emerged advocacy of pupil self-government and school discipline based on democratic assumptions. Much of this change in emphasis has been in response to the political climate in Europe over the past half-century, a climate of fear and apprehension generated first by Fascist and then by Communist totalitarian regimes. In face of this totalitarian threat there have been those who have hypothesized a relationship between child-rearing practices and political regimes:

> the emphasis upon obedience training, the use of severe physical punishment, and a hierarchically arranged interpersonal environment seem to be correlated with an authoritarian political system, whilst emphasis upon training in sharing and co-operative effort, the use of

nonphysical discipline, and a free group environment with no pronounced status distinctions seem to be correlated with an egalitarian political system (Levine, p. 296).

The case for pupil participation in school government in a democracy derives largely from this kind of assumption that the disciplinary and socializing processes of the school are an important source of adult attitudes towards rights and duties, towards political authorities, law and order and the perception of one's capacity to alter the framework of the society in which one lives. In particular, a person's attitude towards authorities and his appetite for freedom has been seen as related to the liberality or otherwise of the disciplinary regime within a school. As A. S. Neill puts it: 'At Summerhill we have proved, I believe, that self-government works ... You cannot have freedom unless children feel completely free to govern their own social life. When there is a boss, there is no real freedom' (p. 59). Pupil participation in school government has been a feature of the Progressive school movement of which Neill's Summerhill is the best known example (see Skidelsky for other examples), a movement itself responsive to the political climate in Europe, especially between two World Wars.

However, it has to be recognized that the government of most schools still approximates to that of the totalitarian state rather than to a democratic model. In many schools the disposition of the principal (and possibly his staff) is quite simply authoritarian. Not only does the question of giving the pupils a measure of self-government never arise, but the problem of political education in any form is rarely considered. Some lip-service may be paid to 'citizenship' and it may even be assumed that acceptable civic values are being learned incidentally, through lessons in history, geography or religious knowledge. But deliberate attempts to practise children in the skills of political life are encountered only rarely.

PUPIL SELF-GOVERNMENT

This inclination towards a totalitarian rather than a democratic form of school management does not always stem from the desire of teachers to exercise personal power for its own sake. There are those who are not indifferent to the claims which a democratic community makes upon schools for the initiation of the young into its ways of government but who feel that in the interests of efficiency they should retain complete autonomy in the management of their schools. An American survey noted the existence of this type of school in which the headmaster conceived the democratic task of his school as providing the fullest opportunity for all types of child and believed that his 'democratic' purposes could best be served by use of dictatorial methods. His school 'was not trying to be dictatorial however. It was merely trying to get a democratic task done efficiently' (Educational Policies Commission, p. 15). More forthright and less confused in his intentions was the English headmaster who replied to a questionnaire about school democracy as follows: 'I have not indulged in pupil councils. I once saw them in operation. I neither wish to produce prigs nor do I expect pupils to relieve me of the task of disciplining them' (Buckley, p. 72).

It is clear that those who feel they bear a special responsibility for order and efficiency in school often take the view that since children are immature and necessarily deficient in appropriate experience, it is inviting disaster to give them any real share in its government. And amongst some educationists there also exists the conviction that not only are there functions which they know they cannot delegate, but that the more perceptive children are aware of this too:

> The whole idea of self-government by children as a preparation for democratic leadership needs a more sceptical approach than it often receives. In the first place there is a fundamental unreality about self-government in schools that certainly does not escape the intelligent child. In very few schools would the vote of the School

Council be capable of bringing about any major change in the school such as the dropping of French from the curriculum (James, p. 68).

It is interesting that this view is shared by the headmaster of one progressive school: 'There is nothing more dishonest than to give people the feeling that it is their decision, when you know it must be your decision.' Quoting this comment, Skidelsky observes: 'Progressive headmasters are very prone to talk about the "right use of freedom", which, in practice, means running the school according to the headmaster's idea of how it should be run.' And he continues, underlining James's point that it is the intelligent child who sees through the deception: 'It is very doubtful whether this type of self-government can work with sophisticated and intelligent children; and although Neill of Summerhill concedes greater latitude than any other headmaster, one reason for the relative success of Summerhill self-government is the youthfulness and naïvety of its citizens' (p. 67).

Although disinclination towards school democracy may be rationalized in this way through appeals to the need for efficient school management, the fear of teachers for their own status and self-respect is also a major hindrance to the development of political education which provides children with practical experiences in government. Buckley's enquiry into 'The Use of Schools as Direct Instruments of Democracy' convinced him that a majority of English headteachers fear to establish pupil self-government 'not because they doubt the resulting good but because they cannot face the change in their traditional position. They feel that any lowering of the artificial barrier between themselves and their pupils would result in a weakening of their authority and a lessening of the awe in which they consider the children should hold them' (p. 147). There is some evidence that this distaste for paedocracy is widespread amongst teachers. Kazamias and Massialas cite a survey of German teacher attitudes towards pupil participation: 'Among those interviewed, there was a fear that political education based on democratic values would have a negative effect on the performance of what they regard to be the fundamental school tasks and on the traditional authority of the teacher' (p. 135). And from the United States: 'We have teachers who sneer at colleagues who try to introduce some democratic living into their classes. They block attempts to arrange any participation by students in the affairs of the school. They proclaim that no little brat is going to tell them what to do' (Kelley, p. 145). Skidelsky, who on the whole took a sceptical view of pupil self-government as he saw it in English progressive schools, concluded that one merit of the system was that it acted as 'a wholesome check on adult pomposity and abuse of powers', in breaking down 'the traditional hostility between staff and pupils' (pp. 61, 63). Given that teachers could overcome their initial insecurity in using liberal disciplinary devices, a move towards school democracy might afford an important bonus in civilizing the atmosphere of schools; although clearly there is no possibility of even tentative experiment in this direction where there exist teacher attitudes towards children as derisory as those cited by Kelley.

The extent to which children are capable of making responsible decisions about the administration of their own affairs is partly an empirical matter upon which most of us have little evidence apart from our experience as teachers. Resolving these divergent views is partly a matter of collecting such evidence. But the apparent differences of opinion amongst educationists stem partly from different value assumptions, partly from conceptual confusion and the level at which the debate about school democracy is carried on. Part of the difficulty about the discussion of pupil self-government lies in the assumption that we are faced simply with exclusive alternatives. In particular, advocacy of school democracy is often couched in extreme language which brooks no sort of compromise (see Neill, loc. cit.) and is based on a conception of freedom in education which begs too many questions. Whether or not it is founded on a fair and adequate reading and assessment of his 'philosophy' and methods, the spectre of A. S. Neill deters many from seriously entertaining the possibility of enlisting children's participation in school government (see Miller, p. 275). Nevertheless, it is tenable to argue that to deny children the right to participate in making decisions about affairs which touch them closely is to pay only lip-service to political education which is democratic. The disturbing feature about the wholesale rejection of the idea and the authoritarian views of the pupil teacher relationship we have just noted, is that these mock the explicit objectives of citizenship training in most democratic states. They reveal the contradiction between our intentions and our practice. We seem to be saying to the young, 'prepare yourself for active, democratic, adult citizenship, but be deferential and obedient as children'.

On the other hand, it is equally evident that children are immature and deficient in the kind of experience necessary to pronounce authoritatively upon the whole range and complexities and imponderables of their own education. It seems that there is something to be said for both points of view—a somewhat lame conclusion which seems to put an end to further discussion and justifies both parties in carrying on much as they always have. In fact, to concede merits in both points of view about pupil democracy is really to say that the two viewpoints bring out different aspects of the problem of political education. Rather than closing the issue, the apparently irreconcilable differences should be the point of departure for a more careful analysis of the problem.

Discussion of the desirability of school democracy rarely begins from the fact that in schools, as in other institutions, there are many different kinds and levels of decision-making. There are decisions to be made about curriculum content and teaching methods. Other decisions relate to the social organization of the school. Some of these organizational matters are central to the educational process itself (problems of grouping and streaming, for example); there is also an area of social organization which is merely peripheral—the timing and organization of breaks and the administration of school meals, for example. The distinction has also to be drawn between intra-curricular and extra-curricular activities. And whilst decisions about all these matters have to be made at the level of the government of the whole school, within this framework different levels of administration exist at the class, house, upper and lower school levels and so on. To ignore the different implications of these and other distinctions is to approach the question of school democracy with a very blunt instrument indeed. For the problem is not simply whether or not administration of the entire school should be put into the hands of its immature members. The question is, given the differences in kind and importance of the decisions which have to be made about the organization of schools, where might children have experiences and insights which make them competent (and perhaps the most competent) to participate? In fact the 'all or nothing' approach to school democracy is itself a function of our disinclination to think of political activity except in parliamentary terms. It seems that, like the state itself, schools are only capable of being governed from the top. And just as in the state the job of governing should be left to those who are chosen to govern, so should schools be free from meddling by those whom we should really be teaching to know their place. But once we free ourselves from this 'total' view of school government and agree that amongst the vast range of policy decisions which have to be made, not all are of equal moment, it is possible to consider how far we can go (or whether we can go any distance at all) and to ask questions about the levels of schooling and areas of school life in which there might be a case for responding

PUPIL SELF-GOVERNMENT

to student initiatives. The question of school democracy does not necessarily hinge (as James supposes it does) on whether the existence of a particular subject in the curriculum ought to depend on a free vote of the school.

School democracy does not necessarily require that children be involved in discussion about curriculum content. Nevertheless, James is probably right in hinting that many of those in sympathy with democratic education would want to draw the line before the point at which children are given the right to determine their curriculum. Perhaps children's co-operation can be enlisted in organizing the extra-curricular life of the school and there is little harm in a school council, where they can air their views on fairly trivial matters of school administration. But the curriculum and teaching methods appear to be in a different category of decision-making. Yet in higher education there are growing student demands to participate (how far and in what sense is rarely made very clear) in the structuring of curricula and examination procedures. The student movement has already filtered down to the secondary school and there is no doubt that schools will soon face a challenge to the sole right of educational authorities to take unilateral decisions about curriculum content.

In fact, so far as pupil participation concerns questions of curriculum, there is probably a good deal of democratic discussion in this area which we do not normally associate with the notion of school democracy. Good teachers display a degree of sensitivity to children's reactions to subject matter and teaching methods which, without being formalized, displays the genuine marks of democratic discussion. Though they might protest any intention to democratize the curriculum, in an important sense they are doing exactly that. The point is developed further below (pp. 60-3). Secondly, even in schools where there is no commitment whatever to democracy, there is usually a recognition that some curriculum options are proper matter for pupil choice. Personal preference is encouraged,

41

whether between subjects or within subjects. Perhaps some subjects, disciplines and skills cannot be put at the mercy of pupil choice; the study of the mother tongue and mathematics, for example. But children are frequently entrusted with choice of modern languages, vocational subjects, the arts and the sports they will take in schools. Projects too are founded on the concept of pupil choice and initiative and the project method was an important part of Dewey's advocacy of education for democracy.

School democracy and the social context of the school

The fact that in some curriculum areas we deny choice, or that once having chosen a subject we insist on children submitting to the discipline it entails, focuses other important considerations affecting pupil participation. These relate to the rights and responsibilities of other parties to the educational situation. A recent Swedish Ministry of Education directive (1969) on school democracy emphasizes that this problem 'should be viewed also from the aspect of staff welfare, as school democracy in the sense here envisaged can, of course, not be established and developed without the collaboration of all those who take part in the daily work at school. Even if pupils must be the central point in the work, there is nevertheless a social relationship of the same character as at any other place of work.' We cannot discuss the government of schools merely by reference to the wishes of those who learn or work there day by day. Pupil rights are often asserted merely against the tyranny of teachers. But teachers themselves are not absolutely free agents in matters of curriculum development or in other areas of school administration. Mathematics and language study (and religion in some countries) are not in the curriculum merely because teachers or educational theorists think they ought to be. Any school principal who tried to dispense with those subjects would find himself under strong pressure from parents, industrialists, educational administrators and others to restore them immediately. Other interested parties press for the compulsory inclusion of different skills and areas of knowledge. So any consideration of children's right to participate in school government has to be set in the context of the claims of other interested parties, including taxpayers. These regard teachers as their agents and some circumscribing of areas of pupil participation must follow from this fact. The community employs teachers as experts, professionals possessing knowledge and skill conferring competence to carry out tasks which it prescribes. The teacher's professional expertise does afford him some freedom of decision in matters of curriculum and teaching method. Some subjects can safely be dispensed with altogether (especially those commonly regarded as 'frills'—the arts, for example) but the community will expect that other skills and subjects have been mastered by children at school. To that extent, a headmaster must retain certain subjects within his curriculum and insist upon the use of methods which have a reasonable chance of promoting set objectives.

The obligation of the headmaster and his staff in the publicly maintained sector of education to act on behalf of the community (if necessary against the whims of students) is true for other areas of school life, not merely those affecting curriculum content. For example, schools are subject to statutory requirements with reference to attendance, safety, health and so on; beyond very narrow limits, for example, a headmaster can no more determine the number of school sessions to be worked a year than can the children in his school or their parents. In at least two respects, therefore, the staff of a school needs to limit the degree of participation by children in school government; in its capacity as experts appointed by the community to perform prescribed tasks, and by virtue of the legal framework within which they have to work. It is pertinent to underline this fact that there are some matters of school policy which children cannot decide because there are some policy areas which even the headmaster and his staff cannot determine. There is a given framework of policy within which the school exists and decision-making must begin from that assumption.

Far from being an impediment to democratic political education, this fact of the necessary limitation upon children's participation can be turned to educational advantage. The knowledge that there are institutional constraints upon freedom of action has to be learned in coming to an understanding of the ways of democratic government. For in this respect the school and its government differ little from other institutions, not excluding the state itself. All associations operate within a social and a legal framework which, at any one time, limits the freedom of members to make absolutely free choices. The government of the state must be exercised within the framework of the constitution, and sovereign states may accept the jurisdiction of supra-national bodies like the United Nations or the Court of International Justice. Similarly, most voluntary associations are subject to the rules of parent associations. A member of a football team may not prevail upon his club to adopt rules inconsistent with those of the Football Association; infringements by sporting clubs of regulations of governing bodies lead to the imposition of fines, relegation to lower leagues and even dismissal from competitive sporting events. A trade union branch may not foster objects which are in conflict with the declared aims of the national body. Some local churches are debarred from using their premises for functions not in accord with the doctrines of the parent church. And all voluntary organizations must operate within the legal framework of the state in avoiding practices which might involve them with the courts. Associations even develop their own procedural rules which act as constraints upon their own members. Thus, to the extent that a school may only determine its own policy in limited areas, it is not in a position inferior to most other associations whose members must accept limits to their complete freedom of action at any given time. This recognition of the limits to individual freedom of action within associations is essential to intelligent political activity. The necessary decisions of school staffs to limit the area of pupil participation in school government can, therefore, be turned to account in underlining this characteristic, which a school has in common with other democratic associations. It is the beginning of wisdom in democratic government to recognize the limitations upon one's activities and to understand the reasons for them. It is not a liberal political education which puts children in thrall to an illusion of democracy as unbridled freedom and leaves them with no sense of their own limitations. Elaborating and rationalizing the constraints imposed upon groups by outside agencies, as well as by the limited competence and experience of their members, whilst emphasizing the strength which may follow from common thought and action aided when necessary by the advice of outside experts, is an achievement of democratic leadership.

School democracy and the rule of law

However, to demonstrate the rights of other parties to the educational situation can be to override all consideration of children's rights. This is especially likely to happen when the legitimate interests of children conflict with those of adults. Consider the kind of situation which is often encountered in urban schools. In an effort to relieve the dismal environment, schools often introduce gardens (sometimes merely a border of flowers around the school perimeter) into the school playground. This is assumed to have a public amenity value in brightening the drab appearance of the locality. And from one point of view it is in the interests of the children themselves, as well as of the general public, to live in an aesthetically satisfying environment. But most urban schools also suffer from restriction of space for children's recreational purposes and the school border or garden can considerably restrain their activities. Damage of these amenities may merely result from the exuberant activity of small children occupied in games which no one would wish to prohibit. And yet, circumstances may be such that to prohibit all contact with the school garden or borders is effectively to prohibit children's play. A 'keep off the garden' or 'no football' rule raises important questions of value and of conflicting interests. If there is no room for both amenities—play space and gardens—it ought not to be axiomatic, as it sometimes is, that the former should suffer. Whether to plant lawns and flower beds (which to the adult may have greater aesthetic merit than a concrete playground) around a school is better than to provide a large unencumbered playground is a matter for discussion. On this there will be two points of view and both should be heard. Some of the 'vandalism' which results to public property is not the consequence of children's wrong-headedness but results from a genuine conflict of interests. Adults are not always sufficiently conscious of the cost of their preferences in terms of the undue restrictions they force on children, or of the protective measures which might be taken to facilitate the pursuit of both interests. To listen to children may be to concede that they have a grievance and open the way to an accommodation which goes some distance towards satisfying all concerned. Recognition of the fact that the children may have a peculiar and legitimate point of view requires only the reasonable assumption that teachers are not omniscient. To admit that children may focus attention on factors in a situation which adults have overlooked is not to conclude that children are equals in wisdom or experience, but merely to recognize that having different experiences they are likely to see different and unfamiliar aspects of a situation. To allow that children may have some contribution to make towards the making of rules

PUPIL SELF-GOVERNMENT

may not only lead to the formulation of rules which are sympathetically observed, but to rules which are more in keeping with the situation which has to be legislated for. When rule-making involves all interested parties there seems a greater likelihood that they will be more relevant to the situation and that children will have an interest in rule-keeping rather than rule-breaking. This is to argue that there will be greater respect for rules which are discussed democratically, and when such rules are broken the punishment which follows may appear just in a way which punishment for breaking arbitrarily imposed rules does not (see Piaget, 1965, p. 368).

In the event, we rarely put these democratic hypotheses to the test. As was argued above, most schools function as autocracies, the rules necessary to the orderly conduct of a class or school being laid down from the top. They take the form of commands. The authority proper to the teacher's status and experience is thought to give him the right to issue rules unilaterally in this way. He knows better than the children what is required by a situation and his prescriptions must operate as commands. But what leads one to question the efficiency of rules made in this way is the frequent reiteration of them which is usually necessary. This autocratic approach to rule-making is open to question precisely because it often fails to produce administration which is efficient or discipline which is orderly. Hence, a justification for securing pupil participation in rule-making would be that the rules required for the proper conduct of the school or class would be better observed if children understood their purpose as a result of being consulted in making them. Piaget puts this point as follows:

> It seemed to us that there existed at least two extreme types of rules and authority—rules due to unilateral respect, and rules due to mutual respect ... The rule of constraint which is bound up with unilateral respect

47

remains external to the child's spirit and does not lead to as effective an obedience as the adult would wish. Rules due to mutual agreement and cooperation, on the contrary, take root inside the child's mind and result in an effective observance in the measure in which they are incorporated in an autonomous will (1965, p. 362).

We rarely pause to consider how far the disciplinary problems characteristic of many secondary schools might significantly be reduced if pupil participation in rule-making were encouraged. The barely suppressed rebellion which smoulders under an authoritarian regime may well give us cause for thinking that one of co-operation would founder in chaos at its inception. But it is an index of how alien to our thinking is the practice of school democracy that we rarely reflect on how far disrespect for the law and its makers (even in the case of the ordinary, non-delinquent child) is perhaps a function of children's never being consulted in rule-making. The widespread adult disassociations of *us* from *them*, as well as the rift between the generations, may well have its origin in attitudes towards rules born in the average school.

The fact that many children appear to have a distaste for discipline and display no respect for rules can be explained in one of two ways. One takes the view that the observed facts are natural facts. This is what children are like; they have a natural disposition towards anarchy. Or one prefers a sociological explanation: respect for rules and authority is a function of the sort of community in which children are reared. There is little experimental evidence to cite in support of this second assumption that it is the sociology of the school which develops respect for rules and discourages rule-breaking. The work of Hargreaves suggests a causal relationship between the social climate of the school and its disciplinary problems. And the well-known research of Lewin and his associates into the effects of different leadership patterns in relation to groups of small boys provides some pointers to the sorts

PUPIL SELF-GOVERNMENT

of responses we might expect from children according to the degree of participation they are permitted in the making of rules. Piaget's work on the development of moral judgments of the child broadly supports Lewin's conclusions that anarchy (the absence of rules and of an identifiable source of these—whether a single authority or a democratic group) is unacceptable to the child. He describes what he calls 'the extraordinary behaviour of boys 10-11' in deferring the start of a game whilst elaborating a complicated set of rules together with criteria for their application and sanctions to be imposed in cases of infringement (1965, p. 50). That is, rules have themselves a function to perform in the moral education of the child. Children expect there to be rules and in situations where these do not exist they will learn to legislate appropriately.

If valid, these conclusions are important for the development of democratic participation in schools. It is a fallacy, countenanced by some well-meaning teachers, that it is truly democratic and conducive to freedom to dispense with rules, or that rules should be as few as possible. But except in the sense that too many rules lead to the worship of procedure for its own sake, there is nothing particularly democratic about refusing to make them when necessary. Indeed, when we speak of the participation of citizens in the making of policy we are referring, in part, to their contribution towards law-making. 'The rule of law' is a fundamental democratic conception. It is of the essence of democracy that laws should be made by citizens or their representatives; that these laws should be widely known and understood; that the amendment, repeal or legislation of laws should not be at the arbitrary whim of authority; and that laws, once enacted, should be enforced without hesitation and without discrimination. It is not the absence of law, but rather the rule of law which is 'the greatest single condition of our freedom, removing from us that great fear which has overshadowed so many communities, the fear of the power of our own government' (Oakeshott, p. 43). Therefore, children are ill prepared for citizenship when adults shrink from this responsibility to legislate within the schools. Nor does it make for efficient administration of the school when adults abdicate their rule-making obligation in this way or, once having made rules, they hesitate to enforce them from a mistaken sense of kindness.

Thus, in considering children's participation in the management of schools, it is important to avoid both the extreme of avoiding the unpleasant task of making and enforcing rules and punishing rule-breakers, and that of concluding that teachers must retain the absolute prerogative to legislate because the alternative seems to be chaos. We forget that like most other worthwhile skills, the skills of democratic government have to be patiently taught and painstakingly learned and that, as Lewin found, the imposition of an authoritarian regime for child discipline is a much quicker and broader highway to an orderly classroom than the slower, rocky, narrow route to school democracy, a road beset with snares and disappointments (see below, pp. 60-1). But ultimately democratic discipline is a happier, civilized and potentially more productive state of order than the alternatives. However, it is not only that democracy is more expedient in the long run. It is also a moral obligation upon the school to bring the young to a state of personal autonomy and self-discipline required of the democratic citizen.

One final conceptual distinction needs to be made explicit in evaluating proposals for pupil participation in school government. We need to distinguish the educational from the intrinsically political reasons for involving pupils in school management. Educationally, pupil participation is a *means* to the end that children should learn the political skills required in the management of human institutions: it is an *instrument* of citizenship training. To implement pupil participation from this educational motive requires that we ask how far, or in what sense, schools and their management are like the institutions beyond the school

PUPIL SELF-GOVERNMENT

which citizens can participate in governing: how far do schools and their constituent groups mirror the structure of the body politic outside? On the other hand, from an intrinsically political point of view, whether children learn any politics is irrelevant. If when inviting children to participate in running the school we are concerned not with education or training (i.e., with the use of school government as a teaching device) but with the political aim of running the school smoothly, efficiently and as fairly as possible, we need not ask questions about the possible carry over of pupil self-government into political behaviour outside the school. Of course, this is a distinction which often is relevant only in principle: in practice, both the educational and the political or management aims might be furthered by a single participant activity on the part of the pupils. But this does not necessarily follow. The sort of device which might best democratize school management —a representative school council, for example—might be an inadequate model for teaching the kind of political participation available to the adult citizen (see Chapter 5 below).

Against this discussion of the constraints on school democracy and of the considerations favouring pupil participation, we may now consider some specific avenues for practical political education within the school.

5
Practical political education

Self-government in private and publicly maintained schools

It is interesting that the most radical and uncompromising experiments in pupil self-government have been made within the private and not the publicly maintained sector of educational systems. Private schools are insulated from scrutiny and pressures of the kind which impose upon tax maintained schools. Parents finance private schools, and those who send their children to progressive schools have usually chosen the school because of its liberal discipline and democratic organization. Moreover, it is difficult to resist the conclusion that pupil self-government in private progressive schools draws much of its *raison d'être* from the fact that these are usually boarding schools. Self-government in these schools is largely a system for airing complaints associated with the managerial and disciplinary problems of residential schools: bedtime problems, dissatisfactions with catering arrangements and problems associated with spare time play activities (see Skidelsky, pp. 63-5; Neill, pp. 53-62). The small size of most progressive private schools is also undoubtedly a factor in facilitating the organization of pupil self-government.

In the past, most publicly maintained school systems have not been much influenced by examples of school democracy from the private sector. Public education authorities have been guarded in their attitudes towards pupil democracy and they have given little active encouragement to the idea of involving children in the management of their schools. But nor have they been discouraging, their stance being one of official neutrality. For example, we have already noted the criticism that English Educational Commissions of Enquiry have ignored this problem despite taking liberal and progressive views of other aspects of education.

Recently, however, some Ministries of Education have taken initiatives in this matter, notably in Scandinavia. In 1968 the Danish Ministry of Education (1969a) circulated 'guiding regulations' to upper secondary schools to encourage the engagement of pupils 'in the organization of the activities of their school', such participation being directed to 'solving problems within practical, disciplinary and educational fields'. Recognizing the absence of proven precedents for this sort of pupil involvement within large publicly provided school systems, the Ministry (1969b) proposed to establish 'a pedagogical centre or school ... for the purpose and experimentation with regard to problems of school democracy and pupil government'. In this school, 'the authority at present vested in the headmaster (rektor) of the school should be transferred to a school assembly in which all pupils, all teachers, and other staff members should have the right of voting.' Finally, 'after a six year period, at the latest, the results of the experimentation should be evaluated, and the Ministry of Education will, after consultation with teachers' organizations and the executive committee at the time, lay down rules for the future administration of the school.' A similar experimental school (the Eiraskole in Stockholm) was designated by the Swedish Ministry of Education following its own similar directive to the authorities of schools and universities to take steps for experimentation in new forms of co-operation between students, teachers and other personnel in education (1969). This directive proposed that the consideration of school democracy should go beyond a review of existing practices and should contain 'an analysis of how democracy functions, e.g., what decisions the pupils have to make and take responsibility for'. As well as questions of school management, 'the forms for pupils' influence in the choice of subject matter, working materials and methods, and in the planning of work, should be examined and analysed for different school levels etc.' The headmaster of the Eiraskole (a primary school) has for some years pioneered the development of school democracy from his conviction that most examples of school government have failed in the past by confining children's participation to trivial peripheral school matters. Thus, in the Eiraskole, the intention is to involve children in discussion of matters central to their own education, and a weekly period is set aside for each class to talk critically with its teacher about the curriculum. In this case there is frank recognition of the psychological barrier which has to be breached when conventionally trained and experienced teachers put themselves in this sort of situation. In Britain and the U.S.A. it is difficult to assess official attitudes towards school democracy in view of the very decentralized character of educational administration in these countries. However, in Britain the late sixties saw the emergence of a student pressure group, the Schools' Action Union campaigning for the democratization of schools, with an all pupil secretariat and administration. Unfortunately, this venture has not established itself nationally, having taken root only in a few urban areas. Perhaps a more serious defect lies in its failure to appeal to working-class pupils and in attracting an exclusively middle-class membership (*New Society*, 26 February 1970; *Guardian*, 22 March 1969, 7 September 1970).

Mock activities

The assumption that real power in the government of the school must be denied to children has led to experiments in political education by inviting them to participate in mock activities: mock elections, parliaments, local government assemblies, courts and even political meetings. These appear to pose no threat either to the efficient management of the schools or to the teacher's role as disciplinarian. Moreover, there seems to be a theatrical quality about these activities which helps to engage the child's interest, even if the activities themselves are modelled upon political institutions from the adult world. The justification for mock activities is that these are play situations which provide lively and dramatic learning situations as substitutes for real political experience. Learning through play has long been respectable in educational theory. Children seem to take quite spontaneously to imitative play. They readily assume the roles of father, mother, teacher, doctor, policeman, shopkeeper and so on. And it is assumed that this sort of role-*playing* teaches children the values, norms and meanings which attach to particular roles and activities.

Two kinds of assumption can be made about the educational (as distinct from the therapeutic) value of children's playing of roles. The first ascribes a present value to this kind of play. In assuming first the role of parent, teacher, doctor, shopkeeper, then that of son (or daughter), pupil, patient, customer, the child learns the appropriate reactions he must make when encountering adults in their different roles. It is also thought that role-playing can be instrumental in developing empathy towards other role-incumbents. A second assumption is that role-playing is anticipatory. In learning the meanings which attach to different roles the child is prepared for possible eventual assumption of these. Thus, as well as learning how to react to adult role-incumbents, he is also learning how to *be* a parent and a worker. How far do these explanations justify the playing of roles in mock political activity?

The main point about roles assumed in the conventional type of mock political activity is that very few pupils directly encounter the corresponding real role-incumbent (congressmen, members of parliament, presidents and prime ministers, judges and so on) in the life outside the school and fewer still are called upon to play such roles in adult life. Making parliamentary speeches, or conducting criminal trials are activities in which only a small number of citizens is involved. In the face of this fact, it is difficult to escape the notion that traditional mock political activities in schools are valuable only in terms of education for political leadership. That is, they may encourage some few of those who participate to believe that they have political ambitions and skills which they ought to cultivate. But for the majority who find public speaking difficult or unsatisfying, the conclusion may be nourished that the citizen's role is essentially passive, except as a very occasional voter, thus reinforcing the quietist conception of citizenship implicit in traditional civics teaching (see pp. 27-31 above). Whilst it is evident that some children—those who are good at them—enjoy mock activities, it is unlikely that all children will. Mock activities place a premium upon the histrionic, theatrical skills. If the majority who lack these are not to remain passive spectators, activities have to be established which call for the different qualities of character, knowledge and skill which, as well as persuasive oratory and argument, are required in political institutions.

However, even if mock parliaments, councils and trials did not have this limitation of failing adequately to reflect the way in which most of us participate in politics, their very nature as play also obscures important relationships between different kinds of political activity. The real weakness of mock activities as instruments of political education lies in the fact that the processes of discussion and decision-making (voting) which they encourage are completely separated from problems of administration: in mock activities, experience of the mechanics of decision-making is divorced from the process of implementing decisions in a responsible way. For example, if mock debates are 'realistic' in the sense of covering topics which are a current preoccupation of local or national assemblies, the decision of the school parliament is quite irrelevant to what the real assembly decides. On the other hand, if the debate is seriously or frivolously concerned with 'reform' of the school (e.g., on the merits of abolishing French or maths, of reducing the school day or week, of providing free biscuits and orange juice during recess) the decision is equally irrelevant to any sort of action which anyone has to take. In either case, discussion is likely to suffer from the absence of a sense of responsibility which springs from having to implement a decision and to live with its consequences. Political education should prompt the learner to reflect upon the likely consequences of his decisions for those who carry them out, especially if, as is desirable, the executant should occasionally be himself. But in mock political activity no one is being asked to *do* anything at all, except talk, and the necessary connection between voting and the consequences of taking decisions is obscured. If discussion is not intended to issue in any kind of action, the deliberations leading to the vote become merely an exercise in speech training or deportment and their value as education for citizenship is significantly diminished. Responsible participation in politics can only result from an awareness of the connection which exists between the making of policy and its execution. Mock activities appear unlikely to cultivate this awareness. Their popularity probably follows from the misconception encouraged by politicians, the press and political theorists alike that voting—the registering of a decision—is the whole or the most significant part of citizenship (see p. 24 above).

A further danger of mock activities lies in their tendency to elevate the procedural aspects of government to a position of importance above the aims and content of political discussion. It is not uncommon for adult business meetings to be strangled by fidelity to procedure. The sense of a meeting is often clear, but an obstructionist minority or individual is able to tie the discussion into procedural knots. Over-emphasis upon procedure in political education is likely to obscure the fact that the procedures of government should serve the people who use them. They are not an unalterable 'given', but instruments devised to facilitate the conduct of meetings. As such they must be abandoned, suspended or modified when they become straitjackets rather than useful procedural clothing. But since a mock debate, by definition, results in decisions of no practical importance (there is no end, only the instruments) it is especially vulnerable to this danger of emphasizing procedural forms, at the expense of content. An associated problem is that the format of debate through which mock activities are usually conducted is a poor training in the procedures of democratic discussion whose aim is the resolution of conflicts of interest, requiring resort to compromise and the recognition of the multi-facetedness of political problems. The scientific character of democracy —aiming at policy decisions through exploring all appropriate data—requires the methodology of discussion rather than debate. Discussion is essentially democratic in character and intention. It is aimed at bringing as many relevant facts as possible to light. Debate lacks this merit. It may be essential in order to carry the debate to conceal what is inconvenient or destructive to one's own argument. It is characterized by conflict. On the other hand, 'discussion is not a battle raised with personal passion for the sake of personal victory. It is co-operative enterprise, conducted for the sake of attaining the greatest possible measure of general agreement' (Barker 1938, p. 28). Whatever mode of practical political training is adopted it is important that it should enshrine the truth-seeking procedures of discussion aimed at achieving concensus, whilst diminishing the ego-centrism and competitiveness which is encouraged in debate.

School councils

Elected school councils are another device employed in

attempting to bring a measure of pupil participation to the administration of the school. The composition of these differs from school to school, especially in the matter of staff representation. This may vary from the mere token presence of a staff watchdog, to staff representation of a size which enables it to exercise a permanent veto over student representatives by outvoting them. Similar wide differences exist in terms of the powers of school councils and their terms of reference. On the one hand they may merely be safety valves where the headteacher or representatives of the staff listen to student grumbles and explain problems *away*. Or the council may be run in a way which provides genuine feedback on legitimate student grievances, and a school staff sincerely desiring to run a school in the best interests of children might improve its own administration considerably through such feedback from a school council (see the *Guardian*, 26 February 1968). At the other extreme are the nearly autonomous student councils of progressive schools. Neill's account of pupil self-government at Summerhill provides a good description of these.

From an educational point of view, school councils are an improvement on mock activities since they can (though they need not) be concerned with matters of real interest and concern for children. Their limitation is in sharing with mock activities a macro-political orientation or what Miller calls 'solidarist conceptions of authority, power and interest' (p. 275). No doubt they do give practice in electoral procedures and the workings of representative government. But, of necessity, few children can function as representatives and, in this sense, they too are instruments of education for leadership rather than devices which might encourage participant attitudes in large numbers of future citizens. For this reason school councils are only useful instruments of political education when supplemented by other devices.

PRACTICAL POLITICAL EDUCATION

The school class

If the number of children who are able to participate in government in school is an important consideration, opportunities for this have to be sought in smaller units within the school. How far does a single class grouping afford opportunities for this?

We have already suggested that in relation to the curriculum this is the level where pupil choice is increasingly encouraged (pp. 41-2 above). In English lessons, for example, a whole class is less likely to be discovered writing on the same essay topic or reading the same work of literature than would have been the case a quarter of a century ago. Much the same would be true of art where fidelity to the ill-defined concept of 'creativity' requires each child to be 'doing his own thing' and ensures that thirty or forty children no longer are set the task of copying geometrical solid objects as exercises in perspective. Student teachers expect visiting examiners to consider it a virtue that they have provided a wide range of class activities amongst which children are encouraged to choose—and better still, that the children have provided the activities themselves. And, as originally envisaged by Dewey (*School and Society*, Ch. 1) the project type of learning situation has the merit of developing entirely from student initiatives. So far as learning situations are increasingly devised on this model, the classroom itself is an important area for pupil participation in the design of the curriculum.

Nevertheless, sceptics argue that though democratic curriculum development of this sort is possible, there is little evidence that these procedures are educationally efficacious, and it is true that there has been little systematic empirical evaluation of the consequences of sharing with children the design of their own curriculum. However, brief reference has already been made to the work of Lewin and his associates which is also relevant to this discussion. Lewin and others created groups of boys engaged in craft activities and submitted these to different kinds of social organization. In turn the groups were submitted to authoritarian, democratic and *laissez-faire* patterns of social control. Authoritarian control required that the objectives and methods adopted by a group were dictated by an adult leader. When organized democratically, appropriate activities and methods developed from group discussion chaired by the leader; this differed from *laissez-fair* organization in which the boys were left to their own devices. This last alternative proved unpopular with the boys and their craft activity was also least productive under this regime. The democratic organization scored over this and the authoritarian groupings in leading to the production of better quality work and being most popular with the boys themselves. Perhaps the most fruitful implication of this series of experiments for the school situation lies in the distinction drawn between a completely liberal or *laissez-faire* situation and the participant democratic groupings where a mature adult encouraged, stimulated and shared in group discussion. Critics of school democracy often simply equate it with a *laissez-faire* situation, carrying implications of anarchy. The Lewin experiments suggest, on the contrary, that teachers wishing to encourage democracy in the classroom are not required to abdicate responsibility for providing the leadership which is implicit in their role and professional competence.

Much the same conclusion would have to be drawn from Turner's account of class democracy in an actual school situation. Hers was not an experiment in child-initiated curriculum design, but covered disciplinary matters in the narrower sense of concern with rules and punishments devised for the orderly conduct of interpersonal relationships within the class. Over a period of time, through class discussion, Turner's six- and seven-year-olds developed a code of class rules and a body of 'case law' and punishments for various misdemeanours.

Although there is not room here to detail Turner's

approach, some of her conclusions underline a number of points relevant to this discussion. First, she avoided any sort of ceremonial procedure or formal organization and merely employed the normal process of class discussion to legislate rules and administer punishments: 'The rules of parliamentary order were never taught as such. This Anglo-Saxon heritage was presented to the group one step at a time, in context, as needed. The children began by imitating the conduct of the teacher, who acted as chairman, which conduct varied little from that of any classroom where the teacher calls upon children individually' (p. 8). Turner also underlines a second point focused by Lewin— the importance of the adult leader in the group, at least in the initial stages:

> The one thing the children appear not to have discovered until it came to them from an adult source was the need for some kind of collective organisation providing a method for handling their problems. This method, whose discovery was the crux of their development, was handed over, bit by bit, by the teacher. The formalities of self-government, the instruments of procedure, were the factors which made the teacher indispensable. Method distinguished group control from mob control. Since it offered the children a satisfactory means of solving their problems they eagerly accepted all that was offered them (p. 10).

As we argued earlier and as Lewin demonstrated, democratic procedures have to be taught. Knowing how to employ these effectively is the culmination of a learning process, not something we can take as a natural endowment of children at the outset. One consequence of this, as with the learning and teaching of any skill, is that the teacher committed to a democratically organized classroom will experience frustrations. The point of the activity will often be misunderstood. Lewin found it much more difficult, and a longer process, to establish democratic control in a group than to set up an authoritarian regime. Thus, as with other

PRACTICAL POLITICAL EDUCATION

curricular and methodological innovations, pupil participation is often abandoned at the first frustrating obstacle, on the grounds that this demonstrates the unreadiness of children for democratic participation. If the teaching of mathematical skill were similarly abandoned at the first hint of difficulty, most of us would never get beyond simple addition. In the mastery of any skill, time is of the essence: 'At the beginning of the second year, the children were able to conduct the meetings themselves under a chairman chosen from among their group though it was still occasionally necessary for me to enter into the discussion' (Turner, p. 5). Moreover, this occasional intervention in the discussion was no impediment to the democratic process:

> The fact that the teacher's experience enables her to contribute more workable suggestions than the children's and to provide them with the vocabulary and tools of democratic procedure gives her a natural prestige in the group. The word to be emphasised is *natural*, since the prestige is a spontaneous thing, based on authority which is intrinsic, not authority imposed because she is teacher. The teacher is a leader in the same sense that some of the children are leaders. The suggestions of the wise teacher will have special value since they are given at times when the children are in need of leadership (p. 7).

Political education and voluntary groups in school

> Suppose we take the focus away from *internal* government—that is, decisions about the way the school should be run—and put it on external actions, actions which the student body can take towards the outside: inter-scholastic competition, expositions, class excursions, parties, community surveys, or work projects. Students can be given a wide range of authority over such activities without endangering the policies or procedures of the school (Coleman in Patterson, p. 297).

For some, focusing in this way on activities outside the

curriculum would be seen as the denial of any intention to educate children in the practice of democracy. However, we have argued that the contexts of legal obligation and community expectations, within which the school functions, imposes necessary limitations on the extent to which the school itself (together with those social groupings—like the class—which are closely related to its central purposes) can be governed democratically by the children. But there do exist voluntary groups of a largely extra-curricular nature which are rarely concerned with the statutory obligations of the school. Within these groups children's participation may be considerable and concerned both with management and the making of policy. The members of a school dramatic society could reasonably expect to participate in choosing plays to be produced, and members of learned societies exercise choice of topics upon which speakers would be invited to address them. Yet the interests and inclinations of children are frequently ignored, even in such modest concerns where they might reasonably be expected to have an informed point of view. Commenting upon the decision of a newly appointed headmaster to break with the tradition of half a century of soccer and impose rugby football upon his school instead, a correspondent to an English national newspaper wrote: 'that the boys themselves are never consulted seems to give point to the widespread belief that democracy in schools should not be allowed to slip out of the history textbooks into the corridors.' Headmasters may feel that they have good reasons for taking such unilateral action. In this case the reason was a particularly poor one from an educational viewpoint alone—'because it is easier to play'. But whatever the reason, the failure in a school to give some degree of choice in a matter of this kind justifies the conclusion that some schools have no intention of training their children to make responsible choices, even in limited areas.

However, given a sincere commitment to the notion that political education requires practice as well as precept, most recreational, sporting, social and academic societies in a school can be made genuine vehicles of democratic government and training. The contributions which pupil members can make to these groups might appear slight and unimportant to adults. Nevertheless, they often exist for purposes which loom large in the lives of individual children and for whom it is of some importance that a school society enables the pursuit of an interest in a particular kind of way, at a level commensurate with his skill and at a reasonably convenient time. Hence, the popularity, the continuity of functioning and the smooth administration of a group may depend upon enlisting children's participation in the making of policy and its execution. For example, the times and dates of meetings are factors about which children's opinions may be crucial in deciding whether a society can function at all, in view of other commitments which they may have both inside and outside school. It is probably insufficiently realized by teachers what a burden of choice a child may carry who has homework to do, who is a valuable member of one or more school societies, who accepts domestic responsibilities and may wish also to belong to some organization outside the school. Learning to weigh the alternative claims of different activities, choosing between them and then committing oneself to them fully, is essential to maturity and requires, in itself, a skill essential to the democratic citizen. The making of these choices by children may be facilitated, and tensions relieved, if they are consulted in the organizing of societies with a view to ascertaining the best conditions of membership and organization. Here real pupil participation is possible and meaningful. And what is important is that they should take part in discussion and the making of decisions: the procedural framework which makes this possible is of secondary importance. Nevertheless, in these voluntary groups, whilst still bearing in mind the need for simplicity and keeping procedures within limits required by the efficient conduct of business, it is probably appropriate to introduce some formality into the proceedings in order to give the members training in the conduct of business and committee membership. The making and keeping of minutes, for example, is essential to the administration of any group concerned with the promotion of practical activities.

Unlike in mock activities, it is in this type of school group that training can be provided which does not merely teach the mechanism of democracy, but which also fosters participation which is responsible (see pp. 56-7 above). Participation in the government of groups existing to foster purposes which children recognize as valuable because they have taken the trouble to join them voluntarily, does enable them to see the consequences of decisions which they themselves have taken: 'It is possible to say truthfully to the members of a school society, once launched on its career, "this is your society, if you cannot organise it, it will fall to bits". Here is responsibility and the penalty of failure, and here accordingly is self-government' (Stewart). In a matter like the management of a drama group wanting to put on public performances of plays, giving responsibility for the choice of plays and their production could drive home, as a mock activity never could, the relationship between making wise or irresponsible decisions and the success or failure of an enterprise of some interest to the child. Yet even if such a project were to collapse through inadequate management, no irreparable damage would be inflicted upon the participants or upon the school. Hence, this practice of allowing the child experience of government in only limited and prescribed areas, acknowledges both his need for real experience of government and also the fact of his inexperience, immaturity, and his being in school primarily to learn from those who do not share these limitations.

But aside from providing some insight into the different consequences of using power wisely or misgoverning groups, does this sort of experience really take us anywhere near the central problems of political education in a democratic society? Some advocates of education for democracy clearly think not. Powell, for example, convinced of the 'desirability of involving children in genuine democratic decision making in order to help them to grasp some of the potentialities of choice and action inherent in democratic procedures', comments scathingly on suggestions that democratic participation can be learned from membership of voluntary groups. He dismisses these as 'boy-scout-type activities designed to assist the indigent', having little relevance to an understanding of 'the political and social structures of the classroom, the school and society'. Like many advocates of school democracy, Powell seems to be advocating much greater participation by children in the sort of intra-mural management of schools we have already discussed. Allowing for the necessary limitations on such participation already outlined, this is a position with which one has some sympathy. However, an additional merit which training in voluntary groups has over involvement in the government of the school is simply that this sort of participation is much more like the kind of thing which adult democracy really is. We have argued that school councils, however seriously viewed by the staff of a school, approximate to the macro, parliamentary concept of democracy. The merit of active participation in voluntary school groups is that this reflects the concept of associational democracy—a notion embodying much more realistically the concrete forms of participation available to the ordinary citizen. At this point, therefore, it is perhaps appropriate to discuss the meaning and to consider the instruments of democracy available to the modern nation state.

6
The meaning of democracy

Democracy in history

Some assumptions about the meaning of democracy have been implicit already in our discussion. We have implied that in some sense democracy involves *all* citizens as rulers: that is, the concept of political equality is part of the justification of democracy. There has also been reference to the notion that political participation involves more than an occasional engagement as a voter with local, national or federal governments. Democracy has been assumed to require the continuous and active involvement of the citizen in the government of his community.

A striking feature in discussions of democracy is the recurrence of the idea that the citizen must be actively involved in the affairs of government. The words 'activity', 'work', 'participation' constantly recur in the literature of the subject. This active criterion of democracy has long historical sanction; to the Greeks who invented the word, democracy signified *activity* on the part of the citizen. Extolling the virtues of Athens in the Funeral Oration, Pericles suggested that in such a state the man who held aloof from public affairs should be regarded 'not as quiet, but as useless'. The democratic man was he who accepted full responsibility for his actions in the sphere not only of private life but also of government. The emphasis was upon responsibility rather than upon rights; upon activity and work: 'the citizen was taken up entirely with public affairs' (Glotz, p. 147). His right to claim citizenship depended upon his willingness to undertake some task in government. Aristotle argued, 'the citizen is a citizen because he does a certain job in the city, and this constitutes his real right to be a citizen' (quoted by Webster, p. 127). A number of commentators have underlined this point that the health of Athenian democracy was secured through the active participation in government of citizens from all classes in the community. It has been estimated that on any given day, one citizen out of every four or five was engaged in some form of public service. In any generation about the same proportion of the citizen body would have the privilege of serving on the executive council. In turn, one member of one of the council's ten sub-committees was chosen by lot each day as its chairman. This office also carried the *ex officio* presidency of the assembly should it be meeting on that day: thus, during the day, the elected citizen was acting head of state, an office to which he had about one chance in ten of succeeding (see Zimmern; Webster; Agard).

In the seventeenth century, democratic sentiment began to revive as the religious ideas of the Reformation were applied to the government of the Puritan sects. Tocqueville argued that 'Puritanism was not merely a religious doctrine, but corresponded in many points with the most absolute democratic and republican theories' (Vol. I, p. 32). Democracy was learned by Englishmen at home and in the colonial settlements of the New World, through the government of the independent dissenting congregations in which each member could take his part. In the colonies especially, the direct, active participation of all citizens in the government of their community was considered essential. There, the democratic implications of Puritanism were underlined by the fact that the colony (i.e., the community) was undifferentiated from the congregation which had removed itself as a body from the religious intolerance of the Old World. Hence, in the virgin political context of the new colonies, the rights and duties in relation to the congregation, which were the prerogative of all the believers, became assimilated to political rights and duties in the management of the community. And when representative government at last replaced direct government by all citizens, it was not from conviction that this was an essential or ideal piece of political machinery, but as an expedient made necessary by the fact of geographical expansion and the practical impossibility of containing all but a few of the body of citizens within an assembly: 'the Knights and the Burgesses sit for themselves and others. What is the reason? Because the room will not hold all of them' (Gooch, p. 103). Tocqueville noted that this tendency towards direct participation in legislation existed in New England down to the nineteenth century: 'sometimes the laws are made by the people in a body, as at Athens: and sometimes its representatives, chosen by universal suffrage, transact business in its name and under its immediate supervision' (Vol. I, p. 57).

A similar confidence in the efficacy of direct involvement of all members in the government of the society was displayed by the early English trade unions, sometimes called 'working men's democracies'. Like the colonial democracies of the New World, these often owed their inspiration to religious dissent, especially Methodism (Wearmouth). And here again, the notion that democratic government must be representative government was by no means axiomatic. Quite the contrary; historians of the trade union movement have noted that even when local trade clubs gave way to national organizations, apparently necessitating the replacement of direct government by some form of representation, there persisted the conviction that *all* members should periodically be responsible for the government of the society. The geographical expansion of the unions' responsibilities was met by 'some remarkable experiments in constitution making'. In some instances responsibility for the management of a whole union was placed consecutively in the hands of one branch after another. As well as the management of their own local affairs, the members residing in a given town were, in turn, called upon to conduct the current business of the whole society: 'the leading idea was not so much to get a government that was representative of the society as to make each section take its turn at the privileges and burdens of administration' (Webb, p. 8). Ultimately the facts of geography were bound to defeat these contrivances to maintain direct participation by members in union government, but it was not until the end of the nineteenth century that union constitutions were deliberately written on the representative model. Representative government was adopted 'slowly, reluctantly and incompletely' (op. cit., p. 11). It was evident that 'the workmen were slow to recognise any other authority than the voices of all concerned' (op. cit., p. 3).

The tenacity with which men have held on to the principle of direct citizen participation in government suggests a loss which they have felt to be involved when resort to representation became necessary: far from being entailed by democratic theory, representative institutions are born of the need to compromise with the changing facts of life. But what sort of direct participation was required in these historical democracies?

For the Athenian it was activity in every sphere of government; legislative, executive and judicial. Even in the last two, an attempt was made by use of the lot, the speedy rotation of offices and a limitation to the number of terms of office which each citizen might hold, to ensure that a high proportion of citizens held office. But it was in the legislature that the citizen could expect full and *continuous* participation in government. In the assembly, policy was discussed and approved in the presence of all. But approval —voting—was the least important activity, being but the culmination of a process in which discussion was the important feature. Sound judgment—of which the vote was the outward expression—could only be made on the basis of a thorough discussion of affairs. Far from believing that prolonged discussion might blunt the appetite for action, Pericles claimed that the Athenians were bolder in action for having paused for reflection. This conviction that discussion was an essential part of democratic government was equally strong in seventeenth-century England; but not discussion for its own sake, or merely as a means of criticizing established authority, essential as that was. Democratic discussion is something more than criticism of authority or mere protest. There has existed the belief that discussion should have a worthwhile product. Discussion was not merely one method amongst others of discovering political truth: it was the only method of discovering some of the things which men needed to know in order to govern themselves (Lindsay, 1929). This method of arriving at the truth by seeking the opinion of all concerned and not simply obtaining the citizen's consent to cut and dried measures, is the crucial activity for the democratic citizen.

A further principle of democratic activity which is of great importance for those who must educate the young citizen is that discussion should be responsible (see above, p. 56). Political discussion sometimes leaves the impression that the participants conceive it to be their right merely to tell *them* what *they* ought to do. And often, *they* are asked to take a multiplicity of actions which are quite incompatible or economically exclusive. Hence, without the willingness to think beyond the vote or the mandate into the practical implications of requiring governments to act in particular ways, there is no guarantee that a decision which emerges from discussion will have any relevance to the situation which really has to be confronted. Therefore, the citizen has not merely to try to imagine himself in the place of those who will have to execute decisions, but has himself to be prepared to assist in carrying out policy decision in however modest a capacity. Failure to realize that this responsibility exists, or failure to accept it when the opportunity occurs, rarely fails to produce the individual who has a facility for articulating extravagant schemes or who is profuse with malicious criticism. It was implicit in the Athenian insistence that offices should rotate in order to give the maximum opportunity for all citizens to hold them, that without this assumption of responsibility democratic debate could be unproductive and dangerous.

This consideration of historical societies which have been called democratic suggests a provisional definition. Democracy requires *direct, active,* and *continuous* citizen *participation* in government through *discussion* and a willingness to *assist responsibly in the administration of policy decisions.*

However, this active definition of democracy has been derived from the examples of democratic government in small communities like the Greek city state and the Puritan congregational settlements of the New World, where government could be carried on by citizens face to face. Except in small utopian communities like the kibbutz (Levine, p. 292) this kind of participant democracy is assumed to have no relevance for the modern world. In the large, modern nation state especially, it is assumed that the citizen must take on a quiet, passive, merely consenting role in relation to government. For this reason, Crick even doubts the wisdom of political education whose slogan is *participation*:

> The less obvious danger of the 'be good boys and girls and participate' kind of teaching is the more insidious: the assumption that participation is both a good thing in itself and the best possible thing. Since personal participation in any sense more meaningful than simply casting a vote is plainly impossible for most people in societies as large as we need to ensure the benefits we demand, it follows that the teaching of participation as an end in itself is only likely to create disillusionment in practice—if it does succeed in influencing attitudes at all and does not simply sound so much cold pie in the classroom (1969, p. 17).

The trouble with Crick's assumption is that participation

is not something towards which the young need to be persuaded in this missionary fashion. On the contrary, 'participation' is their own battle cry, as well as being the desire of many older citizens who become increasingly disenchanted with the voter's simple role of choosing between party programmes which seem to offer only Hobson's Choice and rarely appear designed to come to grips with the chronic problems facing individuals and societies. But Crick's other objection that all but minimal participation must be an illusion is more substantial, and it is necessary to consider how far the classical concept of active, participant democracy can be a model for government in the modern nation state.

The limitations of parliamentary democracy

Since direct, participant democracy of the sort we have seen at work in historical democracies is taken to be impossible in the large nation state, the existence of a freely elected parliament is assumed to guarantee the substance of democracy in the modern world. The right to elect national assemblies appears to be the apogee of democratic citizenship. As we have already noted, education for citizenship has usually been macro-oriented, and teaching the young how to use their votes intelligently is a central aim of political education.

However, parliaments are not themselves uniquely democratic institutions. Parliament is a surviving mediaeval institution which happens to have, as its central activity, discussion of the kind which is essential to democratic government. But even at best, it is a representative assembly which provides no scope for the activity of the individual citizen in the business of government, except in the limited sense and on the infrequent occasions which general elections make possible. If this is the sole outlet for the citizen's activity, then, as L. S. Amery has said of democracy in Britain, it is 'government of the people, for the people, with,

THE MEANING OF DEMOCRACY

but not by, the people' (p. 21). In the parliamentary context the citizen's role is essentially passive; a matter of accepting alternative policies presented to him by parties competing for his vote. Nevertheless, the citizen becomes satisfied (an illusion nourished by political education, which sees voting as the apex of the democratic citizen's privilege and duty) that his representatives do really express his views; that because he gives his consent to such representation in a general election, he is somehow sovereign and this is really what matters in a democracy. And he becomes convinced either that no further contribution is required of him or that none is possible. But this does not satisfy the principle of continuous and active participation in government, which is essential in a democracy. It does not take account of the distinction which has been drawn between 'making the government and government' (Barker, 1906, p. 88). Through parliamentary elections the citizen tends to share only in making the government and whilst this is an important democratic function, it does not contribute towards creative membership of the democratic community.

Thus, it is interesting that two parliamentarians who were members of the British Labour Government in the sixties (the one before, the other following experience as a Cabinet Minister) should have written critically of the alienation of ordinary citizens from the apparatus of government as represented by parliamentary institutions (Crossman; Wedgwood-Benn). Both agree that voting at four-yearly intervals in general elections offers the citizen little sense that government is responsive to his wishes, or that his desire for constructive political participation is being adequately realized (Crossman, p. 21; Wedgwood-Benn, p. 1). In 1956, Crossman saw the solution in reform of parliamentary institutions themselves, including the democratization of political parties. By 1970, Wedgwood-Benn had concluded that we must move 'beyond parliamentary democracy' (p. 23), recognizing the importance of political 'do-it-yourself', as when people respond 'to the pressure of

75

events by binding themselves together with others of like mind to campaign vigorously for what they want' (p. 9). But, as we shall see, this conception of associational democracy has a long and respectable history. Wedgwood-Benn is merely affirming, as a practising politician, the value of a proven method of democratic participation available to the citizen of even the larger democratic state.

Associational democracy

In 1889 an Austrian observer of English political institutions asked 'why in England, without universal suffrage, the working man has long since acquired a greater influence upon the legislation and administration of his country than was the case, at all events until the present day, with the working man on the continent?' He found his answer 'in the voluntary associated life of England' (Baernreither, pp. 6, 100). This tendency towards the achievement of objectives through voluntary associations or *ad hoc* movements directed towards specific objectives, whilst movements seeking to attain these same objectives through parliamentary representation failed, has been noted by other observers of the period. For example, Trade Unions, Friendly and Cooperative Societies, The Working Men's Clubs, The Anti-Corn Law League, the movement for the Ten Hours' Act, all achieved objectives which, beneath ostensible political aims, were at the root of the Chartist agitation for parliamentary reform. Thus, although Chartism was 'rained away' in 1848, this was not a disastrous setback for the British working class. Through membership of voluntary associations, individuals participated directly in the government of areas of national life of crucial importance to their own living standards as well as to national order and well-being.

This form of direct activity in areas of life where the government showed little concern proved an effective school for the development of political self-consciousness amongst those who were denied the franchise. Lord Percy argued that 'in Britain, the political power of the Labour movement was to grow, not out of Chartism with its National Political Unions and Working Men's Associations but out of the craft unions and the co-operative movement, out of groups in which the miner's lodge was hardly distinguishable from the Methodist Circuit Rally' (p. 172). Several historians have documented the educative value of the organization of the Methodist Church and its fertilizing of non-religious organizations in the eighteenth and nineteenth centuries (see Wearmouth, Lindsay). G. D. H. Cole concluded that

> the real democracy that does exist in Great Britain ... is to be found for the most part not in Parliament or in institutions of local government, but in small groups, formal or informal, in which men and women join together out of decent fellowship or for the pursuit of a common social purpose—societies, clubs, churches, and not least, informal neighbourhood groups. It is in these groups and in the capacity to form them swiftly under pressure of immediate needs, that the real spirit of democracy resides (1941, p. 162).

And despite the macro-orientation of much of the American literature on political socialization, there is increasing recognition that voluntary associations are an essential constituent of participant democracy in the United States. Both Greenstein and Hess and Torney have noted the neglect of the role of pressure groups in American political education:

> A citizen who wishes to influence government policies must learn the most efficient ways to make his opinions felt. This problem is complicated by the schools' emphasis upon the formal structure of the governmental process, and the underemphasis on the role of group structures and interactions which constitute a pluralistic society ... The influence of interest and pressure groups

upon government policy is apparently often ignored in public discussion of congressional action and in the school curricula ... the citizen could act more realistically and effectively if he had such information (Hess and Torney, p. 62; and see Greenstein, p. 157).

This neglect of the role of American interest groups is surprising in view of the considerable literature covering at least half a century on group influence in American politics which prompts another writer to conclude: 'To a constantly increasing extent American politics is the politics of organized groups' (Ehrmann quoting Bone; see also Bunzel, pp. 189-90; Kimball and McLellan, pp. 195-200; Kousoulas, p. 162).

Voluntary associations and government

There are three ways in which voluntary associations can be instruments of continuous and active citizen participation in government. Local dramatic societies, football clubs, churches, political parties and groups, labour union branches, learned societies, mother's unions and townswomen's guilds, chambers of commerce, co-operative societies and consumer groups all have their politics. Their members have to make and administer policy decisions: there is legislative and executive work to be done at however modest a level. They can thus help to canalize effectively whatever propensity their members have to participate in governmental activity. Latham noted that 'groups organise for the *self expression* of their members. Even where the group is a benevolent, philanthropic organisation devoted to the improvement of people outside its membership, the work toward this goal, the activity of the organisation, is a means through which members express themselves' (p. 28). It is interesting that Almond and Verba found the highest measure of subjective feeling of being able to exercise political competence in Britain and America

—nations having probably the greatest proliferation of voluntary associations (Ch. 7).

Of course, to call the citizen's participation in the management of local groups of this kind 'political activity' does require a somewhat wider conception of politics and of government than is usually held by the average citizen. Yet this broader conception of political life is quite compatible with the definitions of some political theorists: 'politics is a basic human activity which makes its appearance whenever there are people and rules. It may be seen in small compass in a tennis club or a dramatic society' (Miller, p. 290). Or again, 'politics I take to be the activity of attending to the general arrangements of a set of people whom chance or choice has brought together. In this sense, families, clubs and learned societies have their politics' (Oakeshott, p. 2). On the other hand, perhaps Crick was somewhat scathing about the illusion that significant political participation is possible in the modern nation state (see above, p. 73) because he excludes micro-activity in voluntary groups from the concept of politics:

> common usage may encourage us to talk about politics in the small group—in the trade union, in the office and the family. Some social scientists, perhaps being a little too clever, make quite a song and dance about 'the politics of small groups'. They hope by studying the microcosm to understand the macrocosm. But the difference is not just one of scale: a valuable qualitative distinction is lost. If all discussion, conflict, rivalry, struggle and even conciliation is called politics, then it is forgotten, once more, that politics depends upon some settled order. Small groups are subordinate parts of that order. They may help to create politics, but their internal behaviour is not political simply because their individual function is quite different from that of the state itself. And, unlike the state, they have no acknowledged legal right to use force if all else fails (1964, p. 30).

If having the power over life and death is a necessary

criterion of an institution's title to be designed 'political', then Crick is right to deny that participation in voluntary groups can be political activity. For this reason, perhaps it is not possible to get the feel of macro-politics through micro-political activity: governing the state *is* qualitatively different from governing the local church or tennis club. But the contrary view of Mackenzie also finds an echo in human experience:

> both political scientists and plain men feel that what they meet in the politics of the state turns up again in the politics of the club, the office, the army unit and even the family. What generates political interest in all this range of institutions is that we think we can feel politics in them, and then we cannot describe them adequately without using political concepts (p. 156).

However, the extent to which participation in the government of small groups only nourishes the *illusion* of having political power is beside the point. For the participant value of voluntary associations is not that they are merely substitutes for activity in the larger political arena. Crick, indeed, concedes that voluntary groups 'may help to create politics'—presumably in his larger macro sense of the word. It is important to remember that local associations are frequently affiliated to parent bodies at national level which administer important areas of national life. In Britain, important communal concerns, which elsewhere are often administered centrally by the state, are governed by voluntary associations. There is considerable opportunity for political 'do-it-yourself' at the national level. Some of the most important things in an individual's life are subject wholly or in part to management by groups of citizens in voluntary association. In economic terms, labour and professional associations of employees negotiate the interests of their members with associations of businessmen and industrialists. Only reluctantly does the state regulate this aspect of economic activity where voluntary machinery breaks down. Almost the whole of the cultural and athletic life of the nation is voluntarily provided: where the state or local authority subsidizes these recreational activities, the subsidy is administered through an appropriate voluntary body. In the field of welfare, the development of services tends to assume a pattern of initial voluntary action followed, eventually, by acceptance of responsibility by the state. Education is a specific example of a public service which developed through the efforts of voluntary bodies and which continues to be administered by these (and, to some extent, financed) in partnership with local authorities. In religion, alongside the Established Church, there exist a multitude of denominations, some of them, as Lindsay showed (1934), having hierarchical structures which are excellent models of how the representative system ought to work in a democracy, enabling local congregations to initiate discussion of issues to be taken up at higher levels and possibly becoming the agreed policy of the church. In principle, most national voluntary associations have machinery for policy-making by reference to their membership at the grass roots. They are usually managed by committees of representatives from local and regional associations.

However, as well as the management of their own affairs to promote the health, pleasure, interests and welfare of their members, associations exist within a national community whose character they may wish to shape. Hence, voluntary associations act as lobbies or pressure groups. They seek to bring their influence to bear upon the government of the state. These pressures exerted by institutions may be generated in a number of ways. An association may spontaneously and unilaterally lobby the government in the interests of its members: a particular church may feel that its efforts to provide proper educational facilities are frustrated by the existing levels of grants-in-aid of voluntary schools; pressure to increase the level of subsidy from public funds may result. Or the state may contemplate legislation which threatens the interests of members of an association. The imposition of speed limits on motorways or breathalyser tests calls forth pressure from the motoring organizations. The campaign of the N.U.T. in 1956 against the proposed Teachers' Superannuation Bill is another example of this. Or again, government may contemplate a major policy decision and feel obliged to consult pertinent interests. Royal Commissions and Statutory Advisory Councils are devices for canvassing a wide range of interested opinion. The procedures of Royal Commissions amount to little more than a process of canvassing and evaluating opinions of pertinent pressure groups: they are model examples of how the views of interested groups of citizens are sounded upon matters of public policy. The obligation of the Minister of Education to establish and consult with Advisory Councils was written into the Education Act of 1944. And the major reports of these Councils provide evidence of the number of voluntary bodies which have availed themselves of the right to be heard on educational questions: the Crowther Commission took evidence from 90 groups, Newsom from 61, Robbins from 90 (orally) and 141 (written), Plowden from 143. Much the same is true elsewhere in the British Commonwealth. For example, the Royal (Parent) Commission on Education in the Canadian Province of Quebec received evidence from 247 associations. Heckscher notes that interested groups and organizations are also fully represented on Swedish Royal Commissions (p. 166). Sceptics are apt to conclude that even when evidence from voluntary groups influences the recommendations of official commissions of enquiry, these are more likely to be pigeon-holed than implemented by governments. And there is perhaps little concrete evidence that when Ministers or Departments of State go out of their way to consult interested groups, this is anything more than an exercise in public relations. However, Heckscher also notes that in Sweden 'It is regarded as more or less inevitable that groups of this type and other organisations should exercise a power almost equal to that of parliament and definitely superior to that of parliamentary parties' (p. 170). In Britain, writing of the response to a document (the Green Book) circulated in advance of the 1944 Education Act, Barnard writes:

> the appearance of the 'Green Book' provoked a considerable response from the organisations and authorities which received it, and there followed a spate of memoranda dealing with educational reform issued by organisations of many types—local authorities, political bodies, churches and professional associations. Mr. Butler and Mr. Chuter Ede (the then Minister and his Under-Secretary) gave the fullest consideration to this response, interviewing deputations and touring the country (pp. 43-5).

Implicitly, the views of many voluntary bodies were incorporated within the Education Act of 1944. From the United States, Bunzel comments that 'nowhere is the politics of pluralism more manifest than in education'. He concludes that the school system 'reflects the plural forms and arrangements of American society and the continuous interaction of multiple and diverse political forces' (pp. 190-1).

In general terms, political theorists who have made a special study of voluntary associations acting as pressure groups have concluded that these have considerable influence upon national governments. Lindsay believed that 'some of the most creative political proposals in modern democracy originate not with governments nor with the permanent Civil Service but with public minded voluntary groups, who have a public concern for this or that problem and who have together thought out a remedy for it' (1929, p. 39). And Finer argued that in Britain the contact between associations and Whitehall is 'close, pervasive and continuous ... even intimate'; it is today 'a formal part of the machinery of government' (1958a, pp. 34, 25). As well as merely consulting organized groups, government departments 'often seek an organisation's help in actually *administering* policy' (Finer, 1958b, p. 131). And, from the American context, Snyder and Wilson ask 'how could individual needs be known to government except by formulation through various groups?' (p. 221; see also Key, 1958; Odegard).

Associational democracy and the concept of fraternity

However, pressure group democracy is not without its critics. It has been described as 'a disintegration of democracy'. Zisk notes that from 1900 until 1950 (with two or three notable exceptions) the American approach to interest groups was one of denunciation: 'Interest groups were viewed as interlopers or barriers between citizens and government.' They were 'irresponsible because they were independent of popular control: They were assumed to be all pervasive and powerful' (pp. 4-5). President Truman is reported to have commented that 'It is time to take the government out of the hands of the pressure groups and put it into the hands of the people'. This kind of criticism has also been voiced in other democracies. Raymond Williams refers to 'the unpleasant development of organised pressure groups' (p. 311). Finer admits that 'there are dangers which lead to injustices': the Lobby—as he prefers to call the system of pressure groups—is 'an anonymous empire'; much of its activity is inaccessible to public scrutiny (1958a, pp. 109-33). Lavau notes that in France 'public opinion has been especially polarised and excited about certain pressure groups whose goals are—or seem to be—immoral. For the general public, pressure groups are above all a "mafia" of disreputable hotel keepers, alcohol merchants, supporters of colonial expansion, swindlers or "merchants of death"' (p. 61). La Palombara reports similar uneasiness about the power of interest groups over the Italian government (pp. 8-9). And Powell is presumably attacking this concept of associational democracy when he suggests that democracy must be something more than 'a charade organised by a ruling clique in consultation with a few powerful interest groups' (p. 59).

It would be foolish to deny that the activity of groups is often 'anonymous' with consequences that are anti-social, promoting the interests of the strong against the weak or underprivileged. There *is* a dark side to the activity of pressure groups. Whilst recognizing this, Finer concluded none the less that 'for better or for worse, such self-government as we now enjoy today is one that operates by and through the Lobby' (1958a, p. 107). Similarly, Key argued that 'if the system of organised groups did not exist, it would have to be contrived' (1958, p. 166). And aside from banning voluntary associations altogether (an unacceptable measure so long as freedom of association remains a fundamental democratic norm) the only alternative is to take pressure groups for better *and* for worse and devise programmes for political education which instruct the citizen in these facts of political life, including moral education which asserts the value of fraternity. Ultimately, the problem of unfair pressures which associations exert, is a matter of public education. The innocent bystander may be taught how to associate in order to safeguard his interests. A number of writers have suggested that government by pressure groups is subject to the principle of 'countervailing power'. Some interest groups are defensive in origin, and pressure from one group of interests seems to call forth equally strong counter pressures, an accommodation being eventually achieved which is cognizant of a variety of interests (see Galbraith; Lavau; Finer, 1958b; Key, 1958). Moreover, it is possible to institutionalize this principle of countervaillance so that governments are committed to consulting all available interested parties. In Britain, both capital and labour are represented on statutory bodies like the National

Economic Development Council (Finer, 1958b, p. 131). Castles illustrates the operation in Scandinavia of what he calls the 'consensual relations of the pressure group universe'. Pressure group co-operation in that context tends to produce national economic and welfare policies which are 'accepted by virtually all sections of society' (p. 67). This process of government through orchestration of different interests is one way of securing reform and avoiding injustice. Indeed, obsessed as we are with the merits of parliamentary democracy, we conveniently forget the limitations of the concept of majority rule on which it depends. Pressure groups are simply one way in which a defeated 'minority' may legitimately counter the tyranny of the successful majority, by reminding that majority of minority interests which ought not to be ignored in government legislation. Rather than protesting that a group's representation of a distinctive interest should disqualify it from the great national debate in order to insulate government from interested pressures, it should be widely understood that injustice will be mitigated when *all* citizens know exactly how power is organized and how an impact may be made upon 'the authorities'.

However, it is apparent that some interest groups are weak—the old, the young, the chronically sick and disabled, the badly housed and so on. Even given the operation of countervaillance, is there not a danger that interests of this kind will be ignored as the strong and powerful economic groups selfishly grind out benefits for their own members? At this point it is important to remember the best as well as the worst of which pressure groups are capable. A Canadian writer reminds us of the two sides to this political coin:

> The very phrase Pressure Group had always been anathema to me. Since 'World Refugee Year' I feel differently about it. During that year a few thousand people concentrated on pressuring a few million others. The

result was that large parts of the world awakened to the needs of refugees (Henderson, p. 33).

In most democracies there is no lack of voluntary associations whose primary concern is the welfare of others—the Howard League for Penal Reform, Shelter, the N.S.P.C.C., the Spastics Society, the Samaritans, Oxfam, the Red Cross. Some of these, like the Howard League, are highly respected by the entire community. And the Lobbies organized by Sidney Silverman (against capital punishment), Pat Arrowsmith (for nuclear disarmament) and Martin Luther King, with varying degrees of personal sacrifice, were clearly motivated by concepts of social justice (however little this was shared by their contemporaries) rather than self-interest. Thus, as well as 'interest groups' concerned first of all for the welfare of their own members, there are 'attitude groups' or 'promotional groups' (see Castles; Finer, 1958b). The motivation towards membership of these is disinterested: attitude groups are a means of canalizing idealism, altruism, charitableness. 'Promotional groups exist primarily to advance a cause (Finer, 1958b, p. 117). Even interest groups may have significant subsidiary altruistic motives (Finer, 1958b). The Salvation Army, for example, exists primarily as a means towards the personal salvation of its members; but its social conscience is real and its social service militant. Most churches and many political, cultural and even economic associations have similar subsidiary philanthropic objectives. Thus, an American student of interest groups concludes that

> While these groups, therefore, are pressure groups, that label does not fully define their meanings; indeed, their primary significance cannot be comprehended at all in such terms. Rather they must be understood as representatives of important group interests in American society, and as the bearers of pregnant propositions concerning the meaning of public welfare and the definition of the ends of public policy (Stanley, p. 300).

Several of the national contributors to a comparative study of pressure groups (see Ehrmann) underlined this belief that interest groups cannot with impunity ignore the public interest (e.g., Townsley) and that their existence is not scandalous *a priori* (Lavau).

However, the problem of organizing pressure on behalf of the weak and the underprivileged focuses an important aspect of political education; its necessary concern with the foundation values of democracy. As well as teaching children the language of rights in a democracy and indicating the institutional machinery available for representing personal interests and grievances, it is important to show them the relationship between political participation and moral commitment (see below, p. 112). Examination of the literature of democracy reveals two broadly different assumptions about its nature. One group of writers sees democracy mainly as a political instrument, a mere method of government, not an end in itself but a means to the good life (see Entwistle, 1958, Ch. I): this essay is written primarily from that standpoint. But others have equated democracy with the good life, with the total normative configuration of a society, and have argued that democracy requires social justice, being incompatible with the existence of evils like slavery, poverty, oppression and war. The difficulty with this position lies in its implication that no society ever could be called democratic. On this view, democracy did not exist for the Athenians, nor does it exist today. Given this sort of moral criterion it is doubtful if it ever could exist. But despite these difficulties in equating democracy with a totally just society, it is evident that as men have forged the instruments of democratic government, they have rationalized their activity by reference to a social philosophy compounded of values like freedom, equality, individualism and fraternity, values which have implications for the quality of life as well as for the development of political machinery. Equality, for example, has social and economic implications as well as the distinctly political imperative towards one man one vote. Similarly, fraternity or the brotherhood of man is, historically, an essential component of democratic ideology. The activity of voluntary associations may be aggressive, egoistic, and even a form of social blackmail, unless leavened by some conception of fraternity. From both its theological origins and its philosophical justification in the categorical imperative of Kant, democracy enjoins consideration for the welfare of one's neighbour. Logically, therefore, those same moral imperatives which drive us to teach the young the language of political rights, as embodied in democratic political procedures, also commit us to consideration of the political, social, cultural and economic rights of *others*. It is through the moral dimension of political education that we endeavour to bring home to young citizens, not merely the expedience of voluntary association as a vehicle of political participation, but also the merit of arguments about the public good (see Finer, 1958b; Stanley, loc. cit.) and the potential of associational democracy for promoting philanthropic, disinterested objectives as well as self-interest. Coleman admirably epitomizes this moral dimension of political education. He argues for a need to acquire the

> 'ability to take the role of the other', the ability to internalise others' problems and to modify our own behaviour by taking account of those problems ... Becoming adult politically implies the ability to do this with respect to other *groups*, societies and organizations of which one is not a part—not, of course, to sacrifice one's own group interests to the advantage of the opponent but to 'see the others' point of view', so that compromises may be reached (1960, p. 304; see also Krause on the importance of schools teaching attitudes favourable towards compromise).

Given an awareness of the possible abuse as well as the constructive function of pressure groups, we conclude that associational democracy is the sharpest instrument for ensuring the citizen's active and continuous participation in government.

Associational democracy and government by experts

Some critics of democracy would argue that not only do democracies seem incapable of solving humanity's perennial social problems, but also that this particular form of political organization which values alike the opinion of the wise and the foolish, the educated and the ignorant, the virtuous and the wicked may, indeed, exacerbate society's ills. Since the majority of people may be stupid, avaricious, unjust, lazy or dishonest, government conceived of, for, and by the people may promote the worst rather than the best of human aspirations. Political theorists have reacted to this threat to democracy from human fallibility in two ways. Some (especially left-wing intellectuals between the World Wars—see e.g., Laski, 1933), have argued for the temporary suspension of democratic institutions pending the education of the masses. A second reaction (not in essence very different from the first) is to contend for a government of experts. Specifically, this was a canvassed solution to the problems facing Britain in the late sixties. A cabinet of businessmen, it was argued, would have the sort of know-how necessary to get the British economy moving again. But in much more general terms, it is often maintained that a major problem in modern democracies is posed by the fact that political authorities must make judgments on the basis of expert knowledge which the citizen is unlikely to possess. Modern government seems too complex for the citizen to evaluate political issues, and the complexity of legislation is such that his rights may be infringed or his interests threatened without his realizing that this is happening. In fact, this assumption that it is the complexity of twentieth-century life which disqualifies the citizen from contributing intelligently to government is considerably overplayed. Laski once contrasted the complex problems facing twentieth-century governments with the simple issues facing the nineteenth-century governments, issues which the average man found 'interesting and intelligible without possession of specialised knowledge' and which could be understood 'without excessive intellectual effort' (1933, p. 70). Yet the problems of a fundamentally moral character facing government today —capital punishment, racial discrimination, the emancipation of subject peoples, the growth of gambling and organized crime, drugs, the position of the public schools and the scope of censorship in relation to the arts—are little different from those which Laski thought to be capable of discussion by the average man in the nineteenth century: 'religious toleration, the extension of the suffrage, desirability of a national system of education, the re-organisation of local government' (loc. cit.). On the other hand, some problems of government have always been beyond the competence of the private citizen, however well educated. In the nineteenth century, when welfare expenditure and national budgets were much more modest, the private citizen was even then no more competent to judge the total yield of a given rate of taxation, than he is now able to make similar decisions about what may well be considerably more complicated fiscal problems. These technical details are always necessarily the preoccupation of experts. But this does not mean that we require national assemblies composed of experts. Politics is not simply a technical matter of discovering, scientifically, how to devise institutional means to promote given ends. The *giving* of ends—choosing the sort of community we prefer to inhabit, the definition of the problems which require to be solved and the order of priority amongst these—is the essence of political activity. And in this field there are no experts other than citizens acting with whatever insight and integrity they command. As Crick has argued, we need 'a defence of politics against technology' (1964, Ch. 5).

In this connection it is a further merit of the concept of associational democracy that it helps to resolve the problem of the need for experts in government. Voluntary associations are themselves repositories of considerable expertise; 'the various associations supply the parties, ministries and officials with that technical and specialised advice without which laws would be mere chimeras and administration a mere bundle' (Finer, 1958a, p. 108). For example, the associations which represent various categories of road user—motorists' organizations, labour unions in the transport industry, societies for the prevention of accidents, police federations—should all be repositories of considerable expert knowledge relevant to the development of road construction and transport policy. In pursuit of rational and efficient transport policies, Ministries of Transport should consult the accumulated experience of these bodies, as well as the findings of their own research departments. The same is obviously true of Ministries of Education in relation to associations of teachers, parents, professional bodies, industrialists and so on. Often associations themselves employ experts; but the rank and file member is usually a member because of an interest or competence which fits him to discuss technical questions in a particular context. Thus, the fact that modern government requires considerable expertise does not disqualify the citizen from political activity or argue for a legislature of experts. It merely defines areas where the citizen-in-association can bring peculiar insights to bear in addition to the more general evaluations he must make in the realm of political ends.

Associational democracy and equality

The concept of associational democracy also helps to resolve what is an apparently insoluble dilemma when democratic citizenship is conceived as merely the right of voting occasionally to determine the composition of national assemblies. Lord Bryce once remarked on the problem that the principle of political equality has to confront 'the stubborn fact of Inequality'. In a political context, the concept of equality is peculiarly clothed in paradox. Except in the case of the early colonial democracies in the New World, where, as Tocqueville observed, the principle of equality could derive without contradiction from the fact that the pilgrim settlers *were* both socially and economically equal, advocates of equality have to account not merely for considerable differences in rank and wealth but, apparently, for considerable inequalities in the resources of character, intellect and personality which different individuals bring into the world with them. One may argue that men ought to be equally rewarded for the work they do and that barriers between classes should be broken down, and one might even attempt to legislate in order to institutionalize equality of that kind. But differences in natural endowment are, by definition, beyond the reach of legislatures. To say that men ought to be equal in ability seems merely to reproach their Maker for failing to make them so. It is this apparent fact of inherited inequality which has led to criticism of universal suffrage as a process of 'counting heads irrespective of what is in them': opinions are aggregated rather than weighed or evaluated. The paradox seems to be that in the sphere where equality can be most easily institutionalized—in terms of the universalization of the franchise —either its substance must elude us or else we are committed to the tyranny of rule by a majority whose educability is restricted by a limited inherited ability.

The view of democratic institutions which has already been outlined helps to resolve this paradox. If voting in parliamentary elections is not a major source of political influence for the citizen, these criticisms of the democratic franchise lose much of their force. On the one hand, the apathetic cease to count in a way which they do not if we measure their influence simply in terms of their vote. On the other hand, the fact that in the government of associations we are also concerned with smaller things which are the stuff of daily experience, means that those of limited capacity may make a modest but essential contribution. Burke argued: 'I have never yet seen any plan which has not been mended by the observations of those who were much inferior in understanding to the person who took the lead in the business' (quoted Williams, p. 306).

The conception of equality involved here is not, therefore, a crude equalitarianism, but rather one of equal right to be consulted about matters which touch one closely. There is evidence that historically the demands for equality have rarely amounted to demands for identity of treatment for all men. It is arguable that democratic government has grown, not out of any academic doctrine about the desirability of political equality, but rather from the attempts by men to be rid of the burdens imposed by chronic inequalities of wealth and status. The seventeenth-century Levellers countered the charges of both Cromwell and the King that they had their origin in avarice by expressly denying equalitarian aims. A contemporary commented: 'They are styled Levellers unjustly; they are Levellers only so far as they are against any form of tyranny; equal justice to be impartially distributed to all was the levelling aimed at' (Gooch, pp. 118-19). Historians of the working class movements of the nineteenth century noted that economic equality was not the objective of the workmen's democracies. Far from wanting to secure equal rewards, the workmen were concerned to create countervailing centres of power against the employers and to be consulted about the level of wages and conditions of work: 'Circumstances eating into their vitals rather than the urge and spur of political philosophy goaded working men to agitate for representation in Parliament' (Wearmouth, 1948, p. 30). Isaiah Berlin concludes that what is really at the root of demands for equality is the idea of what is fair: 'the notion of equality and fairness are closely bound up' (p. 320). Hence, in social and economic terms equality expresses itself as a demand for such a redistribution of wealth as will rescue the under-privileged from an existence which is inconsistent with any conception of human dignity or justice. And the political correlate of this is the freedom to create political associations which enable the politically deprived to voice their discontents and work for appropriate remedies. But the sort of contribution which a man will make to the government of his association—and, hence, the meaning of his contribution in the wider political context—will depend upon his own unique personal endowment. Participation in government through voluntary associations enables interest, talent and a sense of responsibility to carry their due weight. According to the strength of his commitment and the number of associations in which he is active, a man's influence can be commensurate with his gifts and his abilities. The more intelligent or responsible have a proportionately greater influence reflecting the wider scope of their interests: they belong to more associations and are more active and influential in these. But even the citizen who is not at home with political and social abstractions, whose skills are of a more practical nature, can make a contribution at his own level of competence. As we have already suggested, in a national debate about transport policy, every different category of road user has a distinctive viewpoint which ought to be heard. As well as the experts at the Ministry of Transport, the private motorist, the truck or taxi driver, the policeman, and the pedestrian all have points of view which stem from different sorts of experience as road users.

Associational democracy thus provides some answer to those who claim that the equalitarian assumptions of democracy find no place for excellence, or that the majority of citizens, having no capacity for abstract thought, are too dull or ill-equipped to understand the intricacy of modern government.

Parliamentary and associational democracy

Although we began by arguing that parliamentary institutions have limitations which the practice of associational democracy helps to remedy, it is now evident that legislatures and voluntary associations have correlative functions in a democracy. National assemblies give legislative expression to the great debate which occurs outside as well as within its walls: 'The legislature referees the group struggle, ratifies the victories of the successful coalitions, and records the terms of the surrenders, compromises and conquests in the form of statutes' (Latham, p. 35). Lindsay believed that 'In a healthy democracy the discussions of the representative assembly will, as it were, act as Chairman for the multifarious informal discussion of the nation as a whole' (1929, p. 42). And Finer concluded that it is in partnership with the institutions of the State that the activities of the Lobby produce a government which is 'honest, humane and just' (1958a, p. 94). However, here we have stressed the importance of the debate *outside* Parliament because this is where most citizens are destined to participate in government, if at all. Our focus has been upon the activity of associations, partly to counter the excessive adulation of parliamentary institutions in traditional political education. Nevertheless, so far as the State provides the legal framework within which all associations function, it does matter that we have the choice between alternative governments which is offered by political parties in congressional and parliamentary elections. The policies of the different political parties may appear to offer us Hobson's Choice in relation to particular political issues. But even if their policies are similar and a citizen has little chance to participate in the articulation of either party's programme, the fact that he may choose an alternative group of men to administer these is an important safeguard against the tyranny of the one party state. To this end it is important that men learn to use their votes in the wider political arena. And even in this matter of the citizen's macro-political activity, membership of voluntary associations can be important. From his study of the relationship between membership of a voluntary association and voting behaviour, Macoby concluded 'that participants (i.e., in an association) were more likely to be voters than were non-participants, they were more likely to remain voters, and they were more likely to become voters if they had been non-voters' (p. 532). Moreover, participation in the voluntary association was the independent variable, that is, 'the causal factor': 'voluntary associations are stimuli which rouse their participants to greater involvement in the political life of the general society' (p. 524-5; see also Almond and Verba, pp. 320-2).

Voluntary associations and social class

In considering the concept of political equality (pp. 92-5 above) it was argued that one virtue of the emphasis upon associational democracy was the fact that through associations a man might make a contribution to government at a level commensurate with his abilities and talents, so that exceptional interests, capacities and political commitment are weighted in a way which they are not if we merely focus upon the democracy of the ballot box. But this virtue has its defect: whilst the citizen of only modest attainment and intellectual capacity can, nevertheless, exert a modest influence upon government proportionate to his gifts, it could be a serious objection to associational democracy that it overweights the influence of the privileged and well-educated. American studies of membership in voluntary associations do underline the fact that it is the socially privileged who are most actively engaged in them. White and Hyman found association membership to be more characteristic of white than negro members of the population and, more generally, to be directly proportionate to socio-economic status as measured by income, home ownership and level of education. From this sort of evidence, Hausknecht concluded that 'the low rate of working class voluntary association membership means that this class does not avail itself of one of the means of political leverage, and as a result is left in a relatively weak position in the power structure'. It seems that if we are committed to a concept of democracy by voluntary association we are confronted yet again with the age-old dilemma that 'to him who has shall be given ...', a judgment that flies in the face of our contemporary conception of social justice.

However, this fact of working class deprivation following from its failure to use voluntary associations has not always been the case. Quite the contrary: historically (as Baernreither noted of nineteenth-century Britain) voluntary association rather than ballot box democracy has been the instrument whereby the working classes have lifted themselves by their own boot-straps out of the degradation of poverty and social and educational deprivation (see pp. 76-7 above) but a current assumption is that these halcyon days of working class self-help are necessarily a thing of the past, paradoxically because of the very success of workingmen's democracy itself. The nineteenth-century working class included people of high intelligence and ability denied access to formal education of all but a very elementary kind. But the democratization of educational opportunity—itself a primary target for the Labour movement—has served to cream the working class of this 'aristocratic' element which taught it to organize and led its associations concerned with the alleviation of social and economic ills: consumer co-operatives, trade unions, friendly societies and educational enterprises of various kinds. Thus, it is assumed that the highly intelligent and articulate working-class leader is becoming a rarity, as the working class hardens into a lumpen mass without ideals, enterprise or leadership.

This somewhat pessimistic conclusion has recently been falsified by developments in the late sixties amongst some of the least privileged groups in large cities. Despairing at the intentions or good faith of elected governments to grapple with the chronic problems of urban life, groups of citizens have organized themselves to come to grips with the complacency of authorities. The proliferation of citizen's committees in the Canadian city of Montreal is a good example of this phenomenon. Some of these groups owe their existence to middle and upper class leadership, as with those sponsored by Saul Alinsky's Industrial Areas Foundation. But other groups represent the spontaneous association of those under-privileged citizens sometimes referred to as marginal groups: 'welfare recipients, the unemployed, workers at the bottom of the pay scale' (*Montreal Star*, 24 July 1970). These 'multifarous citizens' committees' display a great variety of 'origins, aims and methods' (*Montreal Star*, 18 July 1970). Their activities focus on the development of education and problems of public amenities and services in under-privileged areas, especially the deficiencies in housing and medical care; upon problems of leisure and of consumers, resulting in the establishment of food co-operatives (*Montreal Star*, 20 July 1970) reminiscent of the initiatives of the Rochdale weavers in Britain in 1844. Though most of these initiatives have been taken in relation to government and public bodies, one group 'grappled with a private developer, thus presenting in almost pure form the clash that often goes unnoticed between the private citizen and a private company' (*Montreal Star*, 22 July 1970). Notwithstanding the leadership of professional social workers, students and others, it is apparent that the initiative and leadership for these citizen's committees comes increasingly from the poor and under-privileged themselves. As well as instruments of social and political action, the citizen's committees also acquire an educational function in demonstrating the virtues of self-help and the efficacy of voluntary association against governmental indifference or impotence in the face of problems of urban renewal and reform, prompting the conclusion that 'citizen's committees have achieved more for the population ... in ten years than all the politicians put together in seventy-five years' (*Montreal Star*, 23 July 1970). The reader familiar with any British or American city could, no doubt, provide his own examples of this incipient self-help by the underprivileged.

Voluntary association and political education

A frequent complaint against democratic government is that it achieves too little and too late. The citizen's groups just described are a tardy response to intolerable social and economic conditions which threaten to bring North American democracies to the verge of revolution (compare a similar inflamatory situation in Northern Ireland). Is it inevitable that associations for human improvement must await the stimulus of chronic social disease, or can their reformist potential be used to anticipate the conditions necessary for the creation of the good life?

It would be a fair response to this criticism that the democratic processes grind too slowly to argue that no educational system in a democracy has ever seriously entertained the possibility of providing effective political education for the average citizen. The limitations of the traditional approach to civics have already been noted (Chapter 3 above). If the analysis of this chapter is correct—that voluntary association is the most appropriate vehicle for full, active and continuous participation in government—it only underlines the inadequacy of a macro-orientation in political education. Earlier, we broke off our discussion of the possibility of practical political education in the schools, and undertook this presentation of the meaning of democracy in associational terms, at the point where the value of voluntary school groups as instruments of political education was being canvassed (pp. 63-7 above). In the light of the argument of this chapter, the model of the school as a complex of voluntary groups seems more accurately to mirror the polity outside the school than does a conception of school government at the macro-level through a representative school council. Except in so far as this last might draw its representation, in part, from voluntary school groups having a 'real' *raison d'être*, its relevance for management of the school and for the genuine concerns of children might appear as remote as parliamentary government often does to the interests of the average citizen.

Some of the school's constituent groups (class groupings, for example) are closely related to the central purposes of the school. Others parallel the cultural and recreational groupings in the wider community, which exist to further the idiosyncratic interests of their members and which only enter into active relationship with the state when pressing for legislative or executive action presumed crucial to their proper functioning. Some of these parallels between school and adult associations are quite close. Dramatic societies, football clubs and learned societies perform the same function within the school as in the community outside. There are even school parallels of the so-called attitude groups noted above. Some school societies work on behalf of charitable associations, like OXFAM, or promote the ideals of the United Nations' Association. More rarely, but not unknown, there are school branches of the Campaign for Nuclear Disarmament.

These last (attitude or disinterested groups) could be important for development of the concept of fraternity, which is essential for the equitable and humane working of associational democracy (see pp. 84-90 above). Groups which reach outside the school (whether they are affiliated to parent philanthropic bodies, or are *ad hoc* creations in pursuit of local social service to senior citizens, the deprived, the disabled and, however modestly, for engagement in schemes for community renewal and the creation of public amenities) are, arguably, powerful instruments for the development of the sentiment of fraternity. Or as

Coleman puts it, 'It is hard to say precisely what we mean by citizenship or by civic responsibility, but I suggest that such selflessness, such willingness to forego individual interests for a goal of society as a whole, is close to the heart of the matter. And I further suggest that societies of adolescents can, *under the right conditions*, develop such selflessness, such assumption of social responsibilities. It is up to adults to provide the right conditions' (1960, p. 296).

Thus, the encouragement of societies of adolescents in voluntary association within the school could be a more productive source of practical training in democratic citizenship than other exercises in school democracy, whether of a 'mock' or representative nature. But consideration of practical training in responsible government only takes us part of the way towards political education. We have also to ask what steps need to be taken in order that the young may satisfactorily conceptualize their political universe, and this raises the question of the need for some teaching of political theory.

7
Political theory and the curriculum

The primacy of the practical

So far it has been assumed that political education is a practical affair; that children in school should be encouraged to become actively involved in the government of groups to learn *how* to participate in the government of their community. How far, in addition, do they need to learn *that* certain things are the case? Does the theory, as well as the practice, of government need to figure in the school curriculum?

There are several reasons for our earlier stress on practical political education. In part, this was intended as a corrective to the exclusively theoretical orientation of traditional civics. In the past, practical experience of political activity has been denied to most future citizens, and some initiation into the processes of a participant democracy is probably one of our foremost educational needs. We have to recognize the limitations of mere didacticism in political education; the insufficiency of hortatory political theorizing, where we assume that simply telling people the 'facts' of politics and urging them to do their duty is sufficient impetus towards their becoming responsible citizens in the fullness of time. In citizenship training, as with teaching any skill, we have to recognize the importance of learning by doing. The practice of any skill is a necessary condition for understanding how to perform it effectively. There is a tacit component to all our knowledge (see

Polanyi). The most accurate and detailed of theoretical explanations inevitably leaves something missing—often something crucial to the skill. To get to the heart of the matter we have to try things out for ourselves. Familiarly, this is certainly true of learning motor skills, like riding a bicycle or using a wood-chisel, and of intellectual skills, like those involved in arithmetical calculation; but it is no less true of learning the skills of social life, like tact (Price, p. 102) and political skills, like 'the art of exercising public liberty' (Polanyi, p. 54).

A second major reason for emphasizing the practice of politics relates to the problem of developing an accurate and realistic political theory as an explanation of political facts. We argued earlier that traditional civics has often presented an inappropriate model of the processes by which the citizen can become politically involved. As with other areas of theoretical explanation (e.g., educational theory) there is often a gap between the theory of politics and its practice. One way of trying to bridge this theory-practice gap is to emphasize the primacy of the practical; that is, to begin with the practice of politics and derive our explanations of political institutions from examination of the way in which the political system actually works. In his well-known essay on political education, Oakeshott underlined the importance of this fact that political theory derives from the practice of politics:

> The pedigree of every political ideology shows it to be the creature, not of premeditation in advance of political activity, but of meditation upon a manner of politics ... political ideology must be understood, not as an independently premeditated beginning for political activity, but as knowledge (in an abstracted and generalised form) of a traditional manner of attending to the arrangements of a society (pp. 8-9).

However, although political understanding begins in activity rather than in reflection, since the time of the

Greeks, men have been convinced that political activity can be enriched through contemplation. The development of democratic government in Athens led to a new political phenomenon, the spontaneous growth of interest in political theory: 'The average citizen sought guidance and felt the necessity of political education: he was often conscious of his own hopelessness.' As a result 'the rise of democracy in Athens gave birth to the political thinker' (Webster, p. 48). Oakeshott suggests that experience of political activity is not itself a sufficient condition of political education: 'to empiricism must be added a political ideology in order to achieve an adequate concept of political activity'. Hence, 'politics makes a call upon knowledge ... political activity is impossible without a certain kind of knowledge and a certain sort of education' (pp. 3-5).

Another reason for examining the claims of political theory to be included in the curriculum is simply pedagogical. As we have noted, learning by doing is essential to understanding. But it is unnecessary (after the fashion of some advocates of activity in education) and undesirable to suppose that practice is a substitute for knowledge rather than a correlate of knowing. If learning is frustrated without practice, it is frequently hidebound without theory. Mere practical learning is likely to be tied to the situation in which it was learned. It is not readily adaptable to novel situations. Some grasp of basic principle seems necessary if the learner is to see the dynamic implications of the skills he learns. And one source of the discontinuity between theory and the practice of politics is 'the time lag between the period when much of crucial political learning takes place and the time the individual takes on explicitly political roles' (Dawson and Prewitt, p. 86). The consequence of such a lag may be that the adult inherits a somewhat different political universe from that which his schooling described: 'Changes in the international sphere, a new political ideology, and domestic policy changes may alter the political world in a few years and prevent any parent generation from anticipating the political world for which it must fit its youth' (op. cit., p. 87). Thus, if there has only been practical training in a limited political context, or if political theory has been confined to a merely descriptive civics, the citizen may come to maturity with only outdated political attitudes and ideas and with none of the conceptual strategies necessary to bringing and keeping his knowledge up to date.

Having decided that the theory as well as the practice of politics should figure in the school curriculum, the question arises whether it is best taught through the creation of a special subject area, or incidentally through other subjects. Do we need to timetable periods marked 'civics' or 'citizenship' or 'politics', or can we provide adequate political education by identifying politically relevant concepts as we teach religion, English, geography, mathematics and, especially, history? Both these approaches have their advocates and critics.

The incidental approach to political theory

In support of the incidental approach it could be argued that politics is so pervasive of the whole activity of life that the entire curriculum must necessarily contribute knowledge pertinent to political activity. In this view, citizenship is every subject. Thompson has demonstrated the importance for citizenship of much of history, geography and economics where these are taught in schools. Bereday reminds us that even music may contribute towards political socialization through the singing of patriotic songs. Perhaps there is hardly an aspect of the curriculum which is not capable of bearing some political reference and merely to pass through the school system is, willy-nilly, to acquire some kind of political orientation. As we conceded above (Chapter 2), a prime value of the political socialization literature lies in reminding us that political attitudes are a product of every form of social relationship. But as we also claimed, political education implies something more deliberate than this kind of informal socialization. And two specifically pedagogical objections can be raised against settling for political education incidentally through the political reference of other subjects.

First, there is the problem of transfer of learning. Unless, at appropriate points, the incidental approach contains specific reference to the political relevance of data from other subjects, the transfer of insight from a subject context (e.g., history) to the political arena may not occur. There is some evidence that transfer of learning (particularly in the case of the less able learner) will only occur when the transferability of a skill is deliberately and explicitly underlined (Burt). This means that if political insights are to be nurtured through the teaching of other subject areas, these other disciplines must be carefully examined for their political reference and those who teach them must be aware of the political reference of what they teach, accepting the obligation to *use* appropriate concepts as an instrument of political education.

This raises a second objection to incidental political education. The problem of teaching anything incidentally is that in order to achieve the necessary coherence and repetition of subject matter for the 'incidental' purpose (which, from another standpoint, is a major and central objective) violence must be done to existing disciplines with unfortunate consequences for their integrity and for the child's conceptual mastery of them (see Entwistle, 1970, Ch. 6). The subjects we are *using* in order to develop political awareness should, in turn, be nurtured themselves through proper attention to their logical and epistemological priorities. For example, the organization of a history syllabus to ensure the proper development of an understanding of political concepts might be quite at odds with the narrative sequence appropriate to the development of the historical imagination or understanding. Or the insistence on teaching politics incidentally through history may lead to a lopsided history syllabus. It is probably because of the assumption that history provides most of us with whatever understanding of political institutions which we have, that history courses have been overburdened in the past with constitutional history at the expense of other aspects of our cultural past (the artistic, philosophical, scientific, social and economic). Of course, to argue that history in all its breadth should be taught primarily for its general educational values, rather than merely as political education, is not to suggest that a teacher of history ought not to underline explicitly, at opportune points, the implications of what he is teaching for an understanding of politics: as, indeed, the good teacher of any subject will seize opportunities to underline the coherence of different facets of human knowledge by reference to areas of overlap which his subject has with any other (see Entwistle, 1970, pp. 110-16). But the problem of teaching anything incidentally is that appropriately illustrative incidents may occur too rarely for necessary conceptual development to be fostered systematically and adequately. Proper understanding and mastery of facts, concepts and principles requires that these be encountered repeatedly at intervals and in different sorts of context. It is necessary to *arrange* children's encounters with materials at appropriate times and this is difficult on the incidental view of political education. For in an educational context, 'incidental' has a habit of meaning 'haphazard' and there is no more reason why a child's political education should be left to chance than should his mathematical education.

This problem of finding sufficient exemplar situations from other subjects when political theory is taught incidentally is related to a third difficulty in the incidental approach. Quite simply, some of the explanatory concepts which are necessary to political understanding form no part of the traditional curriculum. Where, for example, do we deal with concepts like equality, freedom, individualism and fraternity in the systematic way which does any sort of justice to the complexity of these moral values? (See p. 112 below.) In those educational systems which require the teaching of religion, some attention to concepts of this sort is possible: it is difficult to imagine how one could teach the New Testament without some consideration of the notion of fraternity or the brotherhood of man. And at an appropriately mature stage of development, one might examine the problem of liberty by reference to St Paul's paradoxical notion that one must become a prisoner of Christ in order to be free. But experience suggests that the last thing which is expected to issue from religious teaching is that children should take seriously, as a guide to social and political conduct, the moral imperatives of the New Testament. Traditionally, religious education in schools has often been only too vulnerable to the criticism that religion is an opiate. As with the moral, so with the sociological dimension of political behaviour: this too is likely to be inadequately examined so long as history is the main source of data about political institutions and the social disciplines are excluded from the school curriculum.

The claim that an understanding of political concepts can be satisfactorily derived incidentally from the general curriculum has recently been questioned as a result of a limited, but suggestive, testing of the political concept attainment of some intelligent sixth-formers. Fewer than half of the items on a political vocabulary test were answered correctly by this group, prompting the conclusion that 'the chance tactics of many teachers in the social studies cannot be relied on. The belief that knowledge of politics can be gained incidentally needs to be proved: it is almost certainly a pious hope.' (General Studies Association; see also Thompson, especially pp. 103-4; Heater, p. 140.)

Civics

In the past the failure of political awareness to emerge incidentally from the curriculum has sometimes led to the inclusion of a distinctive subject, civics. This enjoyed considerable vogue in English schools in the years immediately following the Second World War, only to be abandoned in the fifties. Perhaps the weaknesses of the civics curriculum which led to disenchantment were more a function of the concept of democratic citizenship which it enshrined, rather than of anything else (see Ch. 3). Linked to a parliamentary-centred conception of citizenship, civics tended to become a descriptive digest of adult political institutions. It often included a large increment of current affairs also consisting primarily of description of contemporary (and often ephemeral) political and social problems and their solutions. One advocate of civics teaching did, indeed, require that 'the civics lesson be devoted to a *factual summary* of the framework of government of the more important countries of the world' (Buckley, p. 78). 'Factual summary' has an austere ring which confirms some of one's worst fears about traditional civics. Exclusive preoccupation with description (itself a necessary correlate of analysis) usually means that there is little attempt to mediate to the child an understanding of concepts or principles which could find exemplification in his own behaviour, experience or interests. Because political activity is conceived largely in terms of parliamentary affairs, and citizenship is identified with exercising the vote, political education can only be a preparation for something which happens in the distant future. Hence, we can only describe a state of affairs which the child will one day inherit: we cannot be familiarizing him with concepts and principles which explain modes of behaviour forming part of his experience in the present (see pp. 31-3 above).

However, there is no reason why a distinctive area of study (whether called 'civics' or 'politics') should not avoid this tendency towards degeneration into mere description, with its premium upon rote memorization and the likelihood that the descriptions will be forgotten during the period between leaving school and involvement with the apparatus of parliamentary and local government. Indeed, any conception of political education must be judged, in part, by its implications for filling this gap, though the narrowing of this interval in some states (e.g., the United Kingdom and Canada) by reducing the voting age to eighteen, does somewhat ameliorate this problem. The alternative conception of associational democracy as something which can have its origin in the democratically administered groups and societies in schools and which has its substance within the many voluntary associations within the community—thus having considerably more concrete reference for the child than parliamentary institutions—suggests an appropriate curriculum for education in political theory which avoids the disadvantages of traditional civics. In terms of curriculum organization, such a study might best figure as a contribution towards the desirable development of social studies in schools which are rooted in the social disciplines themselves and which attempt to mediate, at a level appropriate to children's experience, the fundamental principles of economics, sociology, ethics, law, politics, social psychology and anthropology. The political content of such a course, in terms appropriate to the child's developing intelligence and drawing concrete exemplar material from his experience, would consist of subject matter which explains the nature of political experience with special reference to the democratic model.

Political theory

'Political science is a subject matter, not an autonomous discipline; it must be eclectic, drawing from old and new' (Crick, 1966). To recognize this multi-disciplinary character of the study of politics is not to argue for an incidental

POLITICAL THEORY AND THE CURRICULUM

approach to political education. It is merely to underline the fact that the logical status of political theory is that of a second order integration of other fundamental explanatory disciplines. However, as our analysis has already implied, the reference of political theory is partly normative and partly empirical. That is, we have to explain how the political system works and explore the most profitable avenues of citizen participation in government: but we have also to evaluate our political institutions for the extent to which they enable us to realize certain democratic values, equality and fraternity, for example (see pp. 84-90 and pp. 92-6 above). And since there is an historical dimension to both our political sociology and our political philosophy, three elements might be expected to figure in any course in political theory.

Political sociology As an empirical discipline, sociology contributes towards explanation of the character of political institutions and the factors involved in their government. This component of a school course would involve the study of democratic political culture along the lines of our examination of the nature of democratic government in Chapter 6. In that context, the argument was that the associational model best captures the spirit as well as the reality of political participation in the modern democratic nation state. The way in which contributions can be made to the management of school groups (see pp. 63-7 above) could be related to the patterns of political participation outside (see pp. 100-2). Almost any current political issue would demonstrate the workings of political lobbies in relation to national governments (see pp. 81-4). Hence, the sociological component of political theory would be designed to demonstrate what political institutions are, how they interrelate and the ways in which people function politically within them.

Ethics and social philosophy Any account of how a political system *does* function should be set within the context of the moral and social ideals by which it is justified and those which it seeks to promote (see pp. 88-9 above). For example, we have considered how far the concept of associational democracy is compatible with assumptions of political equality (pp. 92-5) and have argued that some of the unfortunate manifestations of self-interest which prompts individuals to associate voluntarily in groups can only be mitigated by an emphasis upon the democratic assumptions of fraternity (p. 84). Again it is clear that the justification for voluntary association lies in the concept of freedom of association. In turn, these notions derive from assumptions about the worth and integrity of persons.

However, it is in this realm of values that democratic education is peculiarly vulnerable to the temptation towards a simple, tender-minded didacticism. It is not only that the practice of freedom, equality, fraternity and respect for persons cannot be ensured merely through exhortation: it is also that the relationship between these principles is itself complicated. When applied in particular concrete political situations, different values might point in different practical directions. For example, Collins has shown the practical dilemma, resulting virtually in political impotence, in which fidelity to both the concepts of freedom and equality has put the British Labour Party when confronting the problem of what a Labour government ought to do with the Public Schools. In relation to this same problem of private education, Peters focuses a similar dilemma in trying to satisfy both the principle of equality and that of the equally valid (to him) notion that what is demonstrably excellent in maintaining the quality of life ought not to be destroyed (1966, p. 206). So whatever we teach in schools about the foundation democratic values, we are doing less than justice to this difficult dimension of moral and political education if we merely consider, first one and then another, without acknowledging the problem of interrelationship (amounting sometimes to practical contradiction) which exists between them. Thus, this moral aspect of political education inevitably raises the question of the value and legitimacy of compromise in politics. Indeed, one American student of political education sees the development of a disposition towards compromise as a fundamental task facing the schools (Krause). This notion that compromise is essential to political behaviour has to establish itself against the fact that too many of those of us who teach have, in the past, learned that the language of compromise is near blasphemy—certainly not the language of morals. But obviously the notion of fraternity in politics, for example, implies compromise between the competing interests of powerful groups in the interests of the less fortunate (see pp. 85-6 above).

The rationale of political institutions in moral terms would focus primarily on those values which are central to democratic ideology: liberty, equality, fraternity, individualism, the rule of law. Whether manifestly or only implicitly, a great deal of popular journalism is concerned with the problem of sustaining these values in the life of the community; and the fallacies, ambiguities and paradoxes which arise in discussion of the democratic values could well be illustrated by reference to the mass media, especially the correspondence columns of the press. Use of this sort of material to explore the problem of democratic values should not overtax the intellectual resources of most adolescents in school.

By contrast with democracy and its rationale, totalitarian forms of government and whatever ethical justification can be adduced for these could also be critically examined, although here one is moving into a much more controversial area. Bode argues that 'it is democratic to be authoritarian about democracy' (pp. 214ff). Others are less categorical about the justification for indoctrination, even into the democratic way of life, believing it to be the teacher's function 'to subject even democratic principles to the test of reason' (Spitz, pp. 183-4). In her recent essay, *The Problem of Bias*, Cohen evaluates a number of contributions

POLITICAL THEORY AND THE CURRICULUM

to this discussion of the place of indoctrination with special reference to political education (see also Newmann; Kirk).

History Historical explanation supplies a context for both normative and sociological explanations of political behaviour. Our consideration of the concept of democracy itself has been made by reference to a tradition of political theory and practice reaching back to Ancient Greece (pp. 68-74). This historical reference was helpful in illuminating the kind of behaviour and institutions which men have called democratic, as well as in seeking the meaning of values to which men have appealed in justification of this behaviour. History provides concrete exemplar situations valuable for the understanding of pertinent ethical and sociological abstractions. Oakeshott underlined this concrete value of the study of a political tradition: 'What we are learning to understand is a political tradition, a concrete manner of behaviour. And for this reason it is proper that, at the academic level, the study of politics should be an historical study—not, in the first place, because it is proper to be concerned with the past, but because we need to be concerned with the detail of the concrete. It is true that nothing appears on the present surface of a tradition of political activity which does not have its roots deep in the past, and that not to observe its coming into being is often to be denied the clue to its significance; and for this reason genuine historical study is an indispensable part of political education' (p. 130). As we have already noted, a great deal of history as traditionally taught in schools is the source of most of our power concepts: authority, freedom, justice, equality, magnanimity, monarch, subject, war, peace, revolution and so on. Earlier, reference was made to the work of historians which casts light on the development of democratic institutions in Ancient Greece, in seventeenth-century England and the New World and in the period of nineteenth-century industrialism (see pp. 68-74 above). In the school curriculum, historical data might be used with similar explanatory and illustrative force to provide con-

115

crete exemplars of the political concepts and principles we wish to teach. And since political education involves the forming of attitudes and, ultimately, emotional commitment to a particular ideology (see Almond and Verba, p. 488), this affective dimension of political education might be achieved through reference to the concrete and dramatic examples of human commitment and altruism which the history of democracy reveals. Indeed, one foreign historian of English democracy has described England as 'the *theatre* of a gigantic development of associated life' (Baernreither, p. 11, my italics). The authors of *The Teaching of History* urge that up to the age of fifteen, 'the teacher should consciously attempt to fire the imagination of his pupils and even to exploit the romance of history' (Incorporated Association of Assistant Masters, p. 3). Whitehead referred to a necessary stage of *romance* in the teaching of any subject and one might apply, to political education particularly, his dictum that there is no moral education which does not habitually impart 'a vision of greatness'. But used practically in this way as an instrument of political education, history is divorced from the general purposes of history teaching. We have already made it clear that for the purposes of general, non-political education, history has its separate place in the curriculum, as well as being a necessary component of a course in political theory.

In this chapter we have taken the view that the teaching of political theory in schools is in service of the practical aim of education for citizenship. However, it is important to note that there are political theorists who would question this objective; who see political theorizing as a truth-seeking exercise directed primarily at understanding the body politic, rather than as an instrument of practical politics and politicians (see Miller, pp. 269-77). It is true that the contemporary obsession with 'relevance' in the classroom puts too great a premium upon what is immediately applicable to the practical concerns of life, at the expense of disinterested engagement with knowledge for its intellectual and aesthetic interest. But the opposite danger ought also to concern us when emphasizing the truth-seeking aim of political education; namely, the cultivation of a superior academic detachment ('politics is a dirty game'), the business of politics being left to the practical man who, impatient of all theory, becomes disingenuously pragmatic. Crick argues the importance of not turning one's back on 'the whole tendency of Western civilisation to be an improving, reformist, ameliorative, not simply a contemplative culture' (1964, p. 111). Perhaps we too readily dichotomize the intrinsic and the practical values of education. To understand politics may be to be driven to greater personal participation, if only from the realization that one's dignity and integrity as a person requires active involvement in shaping the social framework, within which even the non-utilitarian and contemplative activities of life have to be pursued.

8

Child development and political education

Just as there are those who doubt the wisdom of involving children in school government, so there will be those who question the feasibility of any possible approach to the teaching of political theory within the school. Oakeshott took the view that at this level

> what is appropriate is something of the character of 'civics' as it used to be taught in schools and the character of its successor in our school education, namely, 'current affairs': an introduction to the current activities of government and to the relevant structures and practices with some attention to the beliefs and opinions which may be held to illuminate them ... not perhaps, a very inspiring study, and in its more dessicated passages ... unlike Greek irregular verbs in holding out no evident promise of better things to come (p. 326).

However, this view that political education in schools is bound to be a tedious, tiresome and unpromising business, accords with Oakeshott's more general conclusion that any schooling is characterized by the fact that 'what is taught must have the qualities of being able to be learned without necessarily being understood' (pp. 315-16; see also Miller, pp. 275-6). Whilst it is no doubt true that in the initial stages of learning anything, much has to be taken on trust, the conclusion that this resigned acceptance of the incomprehensible must characterize schooling ignores many of the gains which have accrued to the child-centred tradition in education. We no longer assume that the child should be submitted to the discipline of rote memorization of meaningless abstractions (see Entwistle, 1970).

Political education as adult education

The assumption that educational experiences should be offered at a time when they have meaning (otherwise, by definition, they cannot be educative) has led to advocacy that political education should be left until the stage of adult education. Livingstone remarked upon the paradox that 'youth studies but cannot act: the adult must act, and has no opportunity for study' (p. 142). And, writing in a political context, Laski criticized the existing social system on the grounds that 'its cure for ignorance has been an educational system which ended for the great mass of people, at the very point where knowledge begins to exercise its fascination' (1942, p. 202).

In this text a developmental concept of political education has been favoured, on the assumption that children themselves have political experiences so that education need not be conceived as preparation for remote adult citizen roles. However, this belief in the possibility of political education with children is not intended to imply that the problem of political education can be solved in the schools. To be effectively developmental some form of political education should bridge the gap between the 'citizen child' and the adult citizen. Livingstone, a persuasive advocate of the need for widespread adult education, was an admirer of the Danish Folk High School, a unique educational institution which contributed so effectively to the political education of young Danish adults, that Livingstone claimed that perhaps Denmark was the really only educated democracy in the world. The principal of one Folk High School has epitomized the distinctive opportunities for political education in late adolescence as follows:

> Youth is the proper time for enlightenment. This is an age of mental awakening when the great questions about life are asked. Then the religious life, the sex life, the feeling for poetry, fatherland and society are fully awake. The soul of the full-grown youth is far more filled with questions than it was during the transitional years and it should be the task of the folk high school to give answers to these questions (Manniche, p. 100).

To modern ears this language may sound somewhat romantic. Nevertheless, it is widely assumed that adolescence is characterized by peculiar emotions, enthusiasms and interests which make it a singularly appropriate time for some educational enterprises.

Political socialization and the child

The belief that adult education provides the only ultimate guarantee of political maturity is no justification for refraining from political education in the schools. Other intellectual, aesthetic, social and moral sensibilities also mature only in adult life, yet we do not conclude that learning and teaching appropriate to these areas of experience has no place in schools. If some of the educational conclusions of political theorists were applied to other disciplines (and there is no reason why they should not be), it would be near impossible for the schools to find a curriculum to teach. Again, since the need for adult education is not widely accepted by adults themselves, one way of stimulating interest in adult political education might be to attempt to provide effective teaching in this area in the schools. But there is also a case for beginning political education earlier than we have in the past which follows from the findings of political socialization research, which was discussed in Chapter 2. There, we noted that the chief value of the research into political socialization lies in emphasizing that children's orientations towards politics occurs much earlier than has often been supposed. And even if the school disavows any manifest intention to educate politically, its disciplinary rituals inevitably inculcate attitudes (e.g., towards authority) which are politically significant. In summarizing the evidence for early socialization, Easton and Hess conclude: 'The truly formative years of the maturing member of a political system would seem to be the years between three and thirteen' (p. 96).

However, it is implicit in the distinction between socialization and education (Chapter 2) that it would be unwise to conclude from this evidence about the early acquisition of political attitudes, that political *education* is possible with the very young. The fact that infants are learning their mother tongue from the first year of life does not prompt the conclusion that we ought to give them lessons in grammar at that time. In the same way, understanding the grammar of politics may be something which only *follows* experience of political activity at however modest a level. In Piagetian terms, the formal-operational encounter with political theory may depend upon some familiarity with concrete political experience. On the other hand, the fact of early political socialization should warn us against the complacent conclusion that political education might safely be postponed until the onset of adolescence. It could be that whatever political sophistication resulted from the later teaching of political theory would only be a thin veneer covering basic attitudes and dispositions acquired in childhood: 'For the most part the identifications and attachments acquired early are intensely and persistently held. They serve as salient categories and reference points that underlie interpretations and relationships with political events, ideas, and objects the individual encounters later in life ... they are altered only as a result of severe pressure' (Dawson and Prewitt, pp. 60-2; see also Easton and Hess; Rieselbach and Balch, p. 74; Levine, p. 286). If political man really *is* this early socialized self, perhaps we should take special care to ensure that these dispositions, skills and attitudes acquired in early childhood are normatively functional for a democratic society. This is to say that, whenever possible, early socialization should be an educational experience. Unfortunately, precisely because it does focus and emphasize the importance of incidental or spontaneous learning, the political socialization research tells us very little about the extent to which early learning of political ideas and attitudes can be a rational process: that is, how far it can be concerned with the development of the rational, autonomous person which democratic ideology requires the citizen to be.

Piaget on political development

It would be reasonable to expect that when we are concerned with political education, developmental psychologists should have more to tell us. But little empirical work exists on the development of political intelligence. The most helpful and suggestive text is Piaget's *The Moral Judgement of the Child*. Whilst much of the more recent socialization literature is concerned with children's perceptions of national authority figures and has little reference to the development of attitudes and skills relevant for the participating democratic citizen, this older text of Piaget does throw light on the problem of children's developing ability to make and alter rules: that is, it is concerned with the development of capacities which are pertinent to active participation in the political system.

Piaget noted that the capacity to make rules, as opposed to faithfully observing rules handed down from adults, emerged at about the age of ten. Before this age, the child sees rules as authoritative prescriptions, unalterable facts of his social universe. In political terminology, the child inhabits a theocracy or gerontocracy, not a democracy: 'These children harbour an almost mystical respect for rules: rules are eternal, due to the authority of parents, of the Gentlemen of the Commune, and even of almighty God' (1965, p. 61; see Hess and Torney, p. 215). At this stage, to attempt to involve a child in rule-making appears to be to ask him to share in the dismantling of a social order which is the guarantee of his identity and personal security. But from the age of ten there is a transformation in the child's perception of his social environment, which Piaget calls 'the discovery of democracy' (1965, pp. 65-76): 'after the age of ten on the average ... consciousness of rules undergoes a complete transformation. Autonomy follows upon heteronomy: the rule of a game appears to the child no longer as an external law, sacred in so far as it is laid down by adults; but the outcome of a free decision and worthy of respect in the measure that it has enlisted mutual consent ... he no longer thinks that everything has been arranged for the best in the past and that the only way of avoiding trouble is by religiously respecting the established order. He believes in the value of experiment in so far as it is sanctioned by collective opinion' (1965, p. 65). This is to say that the child becomes anti- or counter-authoritarian in his expectations: 'From henceforward a rule is conceived as the free pronouncement of the actual individual minds themselves. It is no longer external and coercive: it can be modified and adapted to the tendencies of the group' (1965, p. 70). Piaget's conclusion about the age at which a significant change in moral perceptiveness occurs draws some support from the more recent literature on political socialization. Dawson and Prewitt cite a number of studies in support of their claim that 'the most extensive increase in political learning and in the ability to think and grasp abstractions takes place between ages eleven and thirteen' (p. 52; see also Crick, 1969, p. 49).

On the surface, this evidence suggests the desirability of confining school democracy to the secondary school. It seems pointless to engage the primary school child in rational discussion about rules and their application and administration. Apparently he will take his teacher's word as law: teacher will be one of the unquestioned authorities who makes the moral universe what it is. In face of his disposition to trust authorities, it is sometimes argued that it is pointless to give reasons to the young child. He appears neither to require nor to understand rational explanations of his environment. But there is a difference between a person's capacity for understanding a *particular* explanation of a distinctive phenomenon and his more general awareness of being in a situation to which the giving of reasons is appropriate. We have to learn both the dispositions and attitudes appropriate to rational activity (i.e., the expectation that people should be prepared to offer reasons for what they say and do, and its corollary, that reasons will be expected from ourselves) and the particular rational explanations relevant to different sorts of human activity. There is, on the one hand, the multitude of possible scientific and rational explanations of all sorts of natural and social phenomena in the physical and social sciences. Many such explanations are complex and impossible to understand, even by the well educated who do not happen to be expert in a particular field. On the other hand, there is the understanding of what it means to give scientific or logical explanations of things, and although in practice commitment to rational argument may not be a universal human trait, even the moderately educated know what it means, in principle, to give and listen to reasons. They accept the importance of being reasonable, notwithstanding their knowledge that the logic of many particular reasons will be beyond their comprehension.

It may seem that the second of these levels of rationality is logically prior to the first: that a capacity to understand *particular* reasons for things presupposes the general understanding of what it actually means to give reasons. However, psychologically (as a fact of human learning), it is probable that both manifestations of rationality develop concurrently and are mutually supporting. That is, it is in and through the process of learning and testing particular rational explanations of the environment and of human behaviour that one comes to appreciate, *in a general sense*, what it means to give reasons, and the attractions and satisfactions of the rational life.

As sociologists are increasingly insisting, learning what it means to give and ask for reasons seems to develop out of social intercourse with reason-giving people (see Bernstein, op. cit.; Klein, II, pp. 519-25; Gordon, op. cit.; see Piaget on the social nature of intellectual development, 1960, pp. 124, 238, 281). Whilst rational explanation of any particular command or rule or suggestion given to a child may seem redundant because it is beyond his present level of comprehension, nevertheless, to give such an explanation in reasoned terms could be to assist his habituation to the fact that human intercourse can be a rational activity. The child is initiated, by example, into a particular form of human discourse (the reasonable) rather than another (the categorical, non-explanatory). It is part of neo-Piagetian educational theory that a child's incapacity for a particular mode of intellectual activity (e.g., the mathematical) does not exclude the possibility that some sort of concrete experience will assist in the development of logical modes of thought. And there is no reason to suppose that a form of pre-operational or concrete experience is less likely to assist the development of moral and social conceptualization, than it is in the case of mathematics and the natural sciences. Piaget himself gives some warrant for believing that the development of rational moral attitudes must be fostered in this way: 'Social constraint does not really suffice to "socialise" the child but accentuates its egocentricism. Co-operation, on the other hand, seems to be essentially the social relation which tends to eliminate infantile phenoma' (1965, p. 348).

Some cultures or sub-cultures hardly know what it is for morality to be established on a rational basis. Categorical commands and corporal persuasion alternate inconsistently with affection and 'spoiling' in the discipline of children. Reasons are rarely offered (and to ask for them is 'cheek') and the moral life exists in a vicious cycle where morality is largely a matter of habit or, at most, intuitive. In the context of this sort of socialization, young people may grow up with the assumption that adults have the right to make rules unilaterally without considering the experience or insights of those for whom the rules are made. Piaget concluded that 'it is only in theory that the child of twelve-fourteen can submit all rules to critical examination' (1965, p. 96). And he seems to favour a sociological explanation for the success or failure of our latent capacity for self-government to be realized in practice: 'individual autonomy would seem to be in direct correlation with the morphology and functioning of the group as a whole.' Implicitly, it is possible to live in a social environment which supplies no incentive whatever for the development of moral autonomy. The capacity for rationality appears not to be subject to an automatic process of maturation: it has to be taught if only by example. In any event, when we move from the realms of psychological and sociological theory to the practice of schools, we have already noted the existence of a successful experiment in political education conducted with six-year-olds (see Turner, and pp. 61-3 above). Thus, it is quite possible to conceive of a primary school committed to *explaining* its rules and disciplines, whose ethos and practice helps to lay the basis for the more explicit political education of the secondary school.

Bibliography

ABRAMSON, P., 'The Differential Political Socialisation of English Secondary School Children', *Sociology of Education*, Summer 1967.

ADORNO, T. W. *et al.*, *The Authoritarian Personality*, Harper & Row, 1950.

AGARD, W. R., *What Democracy Meant to the Greeks*, University of North Carolina Press, 1942.

ALMOND, G. A., and VERBA, S., *The Civic Culture*, Princeton University Press, 1963.

AMERY, L. S., *Thoughts on the Constitution*, Oxford University Press, 1964.

BAERNREITHER, J. M., *English Associations of Working Men*, Swan Sonnenschein, 1889.

BARKER, E., *The Political Thought of Plato and Aristotle*, Methuen, 1906.

BARKER, E., *The Citizen's Choice*, Cambridge University Press, 1938.

BARNARD, H. C., *A Short History of English Education*, London University Press, 1947.

BENN, S. I., and PETERS, R. S., *Social Principles in the Democratic State*, 1959, reprinted as *Principles of Political Thought*, The Free Press, New York, 1965.

BEREDAY, G. Z. F., and STRETCH, B. B., 'Political Education in the U.S.A. and the U.S.S.R.', see McLendon.

BERLIN, I., *Proceedings of the Aristotelian Society*, New Series, Vol. LVI, 1947.

BERNSTEIN, B., 'Social Class and Linguistic Development: a Theory of Social Learning', in Halsey, Floud and Anderson, *Education, Economy and Society*, The Free Press, New York, 1961.

BODE, B. H., 'What is the Meaning of Freedom in Education?', in Kerber and Smith.

BIBLIOGRAPHY

BORGEAU, C., *The Rise of Modern Democracy in Old and New England*, Swan Sonnenschein, 1894.

BRUNER, J., *The Process of Education*, Harvard University Press, 1963.

BURT, C., 'The Transfer of Training', *Educational Review*, Vol. 12, 1960.

BRYCE, J., *Modern Democracies* (2 vols), Macmillan, 1921.

BUCKLEY, C. J., 'The Use of Schools as Direct Instruments of Democracy', M.Sc. (Econ.) thesis, University of London, 1948.

BUNZEL, J. H., 'Pressure Groups in Politics and Education', in McLendon.

CASTIGLIONE, B., *The Book of the Courtier* (translated with introduction by G. Bull), Penguin Books, 1967.

CASTLES, F. G., *Pressure Groups and Political Culture*, Routledge & Kegan Paul/Humanities Press, 1967.

COLE, G. D. H., *Europe, Russia and the Future*, Gollancz, 1941(a).

COLE, G. D. H., *British Working Class Politics, 1832-1914*, Routledge & Kegan Paul, 1941(b).

CENTRAL ADVISORY COUNCIL FOR EDUCATION:
15 to 18 (Crowther Report), H.M.S.O., 1959.
Half our Future (Newsom Report), H.M.S.O., 1963.
Higher Education (Robbins Report), H.M.S.O., 1963.
Children and their Primary Schools (Plowden Report), H.M.S.O., 1967.

COHEN, B., 'The Problem of Bias', in Heater.

COLEMAN, J. S., 'A Sociologist Suggests New Perspectives', in Patterson.

COLEMAN., J. S. (ed.), *Education and Political Development*, Princeton University Press, 1965.

COLEMAN, J. S., 'The Political Consequences of Educational Patterns', in Litt.

COLLINS, J. M., 'The Labour Party and the Public Schools: a Conflict of Principles', *British Journal of Educational Studies*, Vol. 17, No. 3, October 1969.

CORDER, A. F., 'Some Dimensions of Anti-democratic Attitudes of High School Youth', in Remmers.

COUNCIL FOR CULTURAL CO-OPERATION, *Civics and European Education*, Council of Europe, 1963.

CRICK, B., *In Defence of Politics*, Penguin Books, 1964.

CRICK, B., 'The Teaching of Political Studies', *New Society*, 3 November 1966.

CRICK, B., 'The Introducing of Politics', in Heater.

CROSBY, C., 'The Study of Political Socialisation in Day Secondary Schools', *Education and Social Science*, Vol. I, No. 3, 1969.

BIBLIOGRAPHY

CROSSMAN, R. H. S., *Socialism and the New Despotism*, Fabian Society Tract 298, 1956.

CROWTHER REPORT, see Central Advisory Council for Education.

DANISH MINISTRY OF EDUCATION, 'Student Government', duplicated, 1 November 1969(a).

DANISH MINISTRY OF EDUCATION, 'Sketch of the "Gymnasium" of the Future', duplicated, 15 December 1969(b).

DAWSON, R. E., and PREWITT, K., *Political Socialisation*, Little, Brown, 1969.

DEWEY, J., *School and Society*, Phoenix Books, 1959.

EASTON, D., and DENNIS, J., *Children in the Political System*, McGraw-Hill, 1969.

EASTON, D., and HESS, R., 'The Child's Political World', in Rieselbach and Balch.

EDUCATIONAL POLICIES COMMISSION, *Learning the Ways of Democracy*, National Educational Association of the U.S.A., 1940.

EHRMANN, H. W. (ed.), *Interest Groups on Four Continents*, University of Pittsburgh Press, 1958.

ELYOT, SIR THOMAS, *The Book Named the Governor* (ed. S. E. Lehmberg), J. M. Dent, 1962.

ENTWISTLE, H., 'A Concept of Democracy and its Implications for Education', M.Ed. thesis, University of Manchester, 1958.

ENTWISTLE, H., 'Educational Theory and the Teaching of Politics', in Heater.

ENTWISTLE, H., *Child-centred Education*, Methuen, 1970.

EYSENCK, J. H., *The Psychology of Politics*, Routledge & Kegan Paul, 1954.

FINER, S. E., *Anonymous Empire*, Pall Mall Press, 1958 (a).

FINER, S. E., 'Interest Groups and the Political Process in Great Britain', see Ehrmann (ed.), 1958 (b).

GALBRAITH, J. K., *American Capitalism*, Penguin Books, 1963.

GARDNER, W., 'Political Socialisation', see Heater.

GENERAL STUDIES ASSOCIATION, Report in *Bulletin*, No. 12, 1968, Longmans.

GLOTZ, G., *The Greeks at Work*, Kegan Paul, Trench, Trubner, 1926.

GOOCH, P., *English Democratic Ideas in the 17th Century*, Cambridge University Press, 1927 (issued by Harper Torchbooks, 1959).

GORDON, J. E., 'The Disadvantaged Pupil', *Irish Journal of Education*, Vol. II, No. 2, 1968.

GREENSTEIN, F. I., *Children and Politics*, Yale University Press, 1965.

GREENSTEIN, F. I., 'The Benevolent Leader: Children's Images of Political Authority', see Litt.

GREENSTEIN, F. I. *et al.*, 'Queen and Prime Minister—the Child's Eye View', *New Society*, 23 October 1969.

BIBLIOGRAPHY

GUILD, N. P., and PALMER, K. T., *Introduction to Politics*, John Wiley, 1968.

HARGREAVES, D. H., *Social Relations in a Secondary School*, Routledge & Kegan Paul, 1967.

HARRISON, J. L., 'The Idea of Education for Leadership', Ph.D. thesis, University of Manchester, 1968.

Harvard Educational Review, special issue, 'Political Socialisation', Vol. 38, No. 3, 1968.

HAUSKNECHT, M., *The Joiners*, Bedminster Press, 1962.

HEATER, D. B. (ed.), *The Teaching of Politics*, Methuen, 1969.

HEATER, D. B., 'The Teaching of Politics in Practice: Teacher Training', in Heater.

HECKSCHER, G., 'Interest Groups in Sweden', in Ehrmann.

HENDERSON, D., *People Have Power*, Harvest House, 1964.

HESS, R. D., and EASTON, T., 'The Child's Changing Image of the President', *Public Opinion Quarterly*, Vol. 24, 1960.

HESS, R. D., and TORNEY, J. V., *The Development of Political Attitudes in Children*, Aldine, 1967.

HESS, R. D., 'Political Socialisation in the Schools', in *Harvard Educational Review*.

HODGETTS, A. B., *What Culture? What Heritage?*, Ontario Institute for Studies in Education, Curriculum Series 5, 1968.

HOLTZMAN, A., *Interest Groups and Lobbying*, Macmillan, 1966.

HORTON, R. E., 'American Freedom and the Values of Youth', in Remmers.

HUTCHINS, R. M., *The Democratic Dilemma*, Almquist & Wicksell, 1952.

HYMAN, H. H., *Political Socialisation*, The Free Press, New York, 1969.

INCORPORATED ASSOCIATION OF ASSISTANT MASTERS, *The Teaching of History*, Cambridge University Press, 1957.

JACKSON, R., 'Children's Political Choices', *Education and Social Science*, Vol. I, No. 4, 1970.

JAMES, E., *Education for Leadership*, Harrap, 1951.

JENNINGS, M. K., and NIEMI, R. G., *Patterns of Political Learning*, see *Harvard Educational Review*.

KARIEL, H. S., *The Promise of Politics*, Prentice-Hall, 1966.

KAZAMIAS, A. M., and MASSIALAS, B. G., *Tradition and Change in Education*, Prentice-Hall, 1965.

KEETON, G. W., *The Passing of Parliament*, E. Benn, 1954.

KELLEY, E. C., 'The Importance of Education for Citizenship', see Westley-Gibson.

KERBER, A., and SMITH, W. R. (eds.), *Educational Issues in a Changing Society*, Wayne State University Press, 1968.

KEY, V. O., *Politics, Parties and Pressure Groups*, Thomas Y. Cromwell, 1958.

BIBLIOGRAPHY

KEY, V. O., *Public Opinion and American Democracy*, Alfred A. Knopf, 1964.

KIMBALL, S. T., and MCLELLAN, J. E., *Education and the New America*, Vintage Books, 1962.

KIRK, R., Discussion paper in *Harvard Educational Review*.

KIRSCH, A. D., 'Social Distance and Some Related Variables in Voting Behaviour', in Remmers (ed.).

KLEIN, J., *Samples from English Culture*, Vol. II, Routledge & Kegan Paul, 1965.

KOUSOULAS, D. G., *On Government*, Wadsworth, 1968.

KRAUSE, M. S., *A Logic of Civic Education*, Research Report of Institute for Juvenile Research, Chicago, 1970.

LANE, R. E., 'Political Education in the Midst of Life's Struggles', in *Harvard Educational Review*.

LA PALOMBARA, J., *Interest Groups in Italian Politics*, Princeton University Press, 1964.

LASKI, H. J., *Democracy in Crisis*, Allen & Unwin, 1933.

LASKI, H. J., *Reflections on the Revolution of Our Time*, Allen & Unwin, 1942.

LATHAM, E., *The Group Basis of Politics*, Octagon Books, 1965.

LAVAU, G., 'Political Pressure by Interest Groups in France', in Ehrmann.

LEVINE, R., 'Political Socialisation and Cultural Change', in *Old Societies and New States*, Geertz C. (ed.), The Free Press, New York, 1963.

LEWIN, K., *Resolving Social Conflicts*, Harper, 1948.

LINDSAY, A. D., *The Essentials of Democracy*, Oxford University Press, 1929.

LINDSAY, A. D., *The Churches and Democracy*, Oxford University Press, 1934.

LINDSAY, A. D., *The Modern Democratic State*, Oxford University Press, 1943.

LIPSET, S. M., 'Some Social Requisites of Democracy: Economic Development and Political Legitimacy', *American Political Science Review*, Vol. LIII, 1959.

LITT, E. (ed.), *The Political Imagination*, Scott, Foresman, 1966.

LIVINGSTONE, R., *Education for a World Adrift*, Cambridge University Press, 1943.

MACCOBY, H., 'The Differential Political Activity of Participants in a Voluntary Association', *American Sociological Review*, Vol. 23, No. 5, 1958.

MACKENZIE, W. J. M., *Politics and Social Science*, Penguin Books, 1967.

MCLENDON, J. C. (ed.), *Social Foundations of Education*, Macmillan, 1966.

BIBLIOGRAPHY

MAINER, R. E., 'Attitude Change in Inter-group Education Programs', in Remmers.

MANNICHE, P., *Living Democracy in Denmark*, G.E.C. Gad, 1952.

MERRIAM, C. E., *The Making of Citizens*, Teachers' College Press, 1966.

MILLER, J. D. B., *The Nature of Politics*, Penguin Books, 1962.

MINISTRY OF EDUCATION, *Citizens Growing Up*, H.M.S.O. 1949.

Montreal Star, 18, 20 and 21 to 24 July 1970.

NEILL, A. S., *Summerhill*, Penguin Books, 1968.

NEWMANN, F. M., Discussion paper in *Harvard Educational Review*.

NEWSOM REPORT, see Central Advisory Council for Education.

OAKESHOTT, M., *Rationalism in Politics and Other Essays*, Methuen, 1962.

ODEGARD, P. H., *Pressure Politics*, Columbia University Press, 1928 (reprinted by University Microfilm Inc., Ann Arbor, 1966).

PARENT REPORT, *Report of the Royal Commission of Inquiry on Education in the Province of Quebec*, Quebec Official Printer, 1963.

PATTERSON, F. (ed.), *The Adolescent Citizen*, Free Press, Chicago, 1960.

PATTERSON, F., 'The Changing Image of Secondary Education' and 'Citizenship and the High School', in Patterson.

PATTERSON, F., 'Political Reality in Childhood', in Raths and Grambs.

PAULSTON, R. G., *Educational Change in Sweden*, Teachers' College Press, 1968.

PERCY, LORD EUSTACE, *The Heresy of Democracy*, Eyre & Spottiswoode, 1954.

PETERS, R. S., *Ethics and Education*, Allen & Unwin, 1966.

PIAGET, J., *The Language and Thought of the Child*, Routledge & Kegan Paul, 1960.

PIAGET, J., *The Child's Conception of the World*, Routledge & Kegan Paul, 1967.

PIAGET, J., *The Moral Judgment of the Child*, Routledge & Kegan Paul, 1968.

PLOWDEN REPORT, see Central Advisory Council for Education.

POLANYI, M., *Personal Knowledge*, Routledge & Kegan Paul, 1958.

POWELL, J. P., 'On Justifying a Broad Educational Curriculum', *Educational Philosophy and Theory*, Vol. 2, No. 1, 1970.

PRICE, H. H., *Thinking and Experience*, Hutchinson's University Library, 1969.

QUINTILIAN, 'Institutio Oratorio' in *Quintilian on Education* (translated and with introduction by W. H. Smail), Clarendon Press, 1938.

BIBLIOGRAPHY

RATHS, J. D., and GRAMBS, J. D. (eds.), *Society and Education*, Prentice-Hall, 1965.

REMMERS, H. H. (ed.), *Anti-Democratic Attitudes in American Schools*, Northwestern University Press, 1963.

RIESELBACH, L. N., and BALCH, G. I. (eds.), *Psychology and Politics*, Holt, Reinhart & Winston, 1969.

ROBBINS REPORT, see Central Advisory Council for Education.

ROBSON, W. A., *Politics and Government*, Allen & Unwin, 1967.

SCOTT, A. M., and HUNT, M. A., *Congress and Lobbies: Image and Reality*, University of North Carolina Press, 1965.

SCOTT, J. C., 'Membership and Participation in Voluntary Associations', *American Sociological Review*, Vol. 22, No. 3, 1957.

SIGEL, R., 'Assumptions about the Learning of Political Values', in Rieselbach and Balch.

SKIDELSKY, R., *English Progressive Schools*, Penguin Books, 1969.

SNYDER, R. C., and WILSON, H. H., *The Roots of Political Behaviour*, American Book Co., 1949.

SPITZ, D., *Politics, Patriotism and the Teacher*, in McLendon.

STANLEY, W. O., 'Organised Interests and Social Power', in Kerber and Smith.

STEWART, M., paper in *Education for Citizenship in Secondary Schools*, Association for Education in Citizenship, 1935.

SWEDISH MINISTRY OF EDUCATION, 'The Participation of Youth in Present Day Society', duplicated, 14 February 1969.

TANSEY, P. J., and UNWIN, D., *Simulation and Gaming in Education*, Methuen Educational, 1969.

THOMPSON, C., 'The Teaching of Politics in Practice: School', in Heater.

TOCQUEVILLE, A. DE, *Democracy in America*, 2 vols., Knopf, 1946, revised ed.

TOWNSLEY, W. A., 'Pressure Groups in Australia', in Ehrmann.

TURNER, M. E., *The Child within the Group: an Experiment in Self-government*, Stanford University Press, 1957.

WEARMOUTH, R. F., *Methodism and the Working Class Movement in England, 1800-50*, Epworth Press, 1937.

WEARMOUTH, R. F., *Methodism and the Common People of the 18th Century*, Epworth Press, 1945.

WEARMOUTH, R. F., *Some Working Class Movements of the 19th Century*, Epworth Press, 1948.

WEBB, S., and WEBB, B., *History of Trade Unionism*, Longmans, Green, 1920.

WEBSTER, T. B. L., *Political Interpretations in Greek Literature*, Manchester University Press, 1948.

WEDGWOOD-BENN, A., *The New Politics*, Fabian Society Tract 402, 1970.

BIBLIOGRAPHY

WEINER, M., *The Politics of Scarcity: Public Pressure and Political Response in India*, University of Chicago Press, 1962.

WESTLEY-GIBSON, D. (ed.), *Social Foundations of Education*, The Free Press, New York, 1967.

WHITE, J., 'Instruction in Obedience', *New Society*, May 1968.

WHITEHEAD, A. N., *The Aims of Education*, Williams & Norgate, 1955.

WILLIAMS, R., *The Long Revolution*, Chatto & Windus, 1961.

WRIGHT, C. R., and HYMAN, H. H., 'Voluntary Association Membership of American Adults', *American Sociological Review*, Vol. 23, No. 3, 1958.

ZEIGLER, H., *Interest Groups in American Society*, Prentice-Hall, 1964.

ZIMMER, B. G., and HAWLEY, A. H., 'The Significance of Membership in Associations', *American Journal of Sociology*, Vol. LXV, No. 2, 1959.

ZIMMERN, A., *The Greek Commonwealth*, Oxford University Press, 1931.

ZISK, B. H. (ed.), *American Political Interest Groups*, Wadsworth, 1969.

Suggestions for further reading

Many of the references in the text provide hints to further reading, but it may be helpful to focus on those bibliographical items which bear most closely on the argument of the book. (All items noted below are listed in the bibliography.)

This text is a shortened and updated version of my own thesis (1958) and additional documentation of many of the points raised in the present text can be found there, especially in relation to the problem of defining democracy and the historical development of democratic institutions and values. Zimmern, Webster, Agard and Glotz provide analyses of Greek democracy, Gooch and Borgeaud of the origins of democracy in seventeenth-century England and America, Wearmouth and Lindsay (1934) of the relationship between religious denominations and democracy, and Baernreither, Cole (1941b) and the Webbs on workingmen's democracies in nineteenth-century England.

Criticism of parliamentary democracy is developed by Keeton, Crossman and Wedgwood-Benn. Of the growing literature of associational or pressure group democracy, Finer's (1958a) is a readable and critical but sympathetic account of the Lobby in Britain, whilst Key (1958), Zeigler and Holtzman provide surveys of the American situation. Ehrmann (ed.) and Castles are comparative studies of interest or pressure groups. Castles is a briefer, less descriptive study, providing a classification of groups and their in-

SUGGESTIONS FOR FURTHER READING

fluence and growth in different kinds of political system.

For an analysis of the foundation values of democracy—equality, freedom, fraternity, respect for persons (as well as the concept of democracy itself)—see Peters (also Benn and Peters). Peters also outlines a concept of education which I have had in mind when distinguishing education from socialization in Chapter 2. See also Easton and Dennis (esp. Ch. 2) on the ambiguity and normative assumptions of the terms 'stability' and 'socialization' in much of the literature of political socialization.

The growing literature of political socialization is well summarized by Dawson and Prewitt, and briefly by Gardner. Whilst some of this socialization literature is pertinent to our discussion of the age at which schools ought to offer political education, Piaget (1965) still seems a more fruitful point of departure for consideration of this topic.